Cooking with the Horse and Buggy People Series

horse and buggy Montana

THE FOOD OF THE AMISH COMMUNITY IN ST. IGNATIUS, MONTANA

compiled by Amy Engbretson and Emily Troyer

First Printing, April 2012

ISBN 978-1-933753-225

Cover Photo: Bruce Hochstetler
Food Styling: Rosetta Wengerd
Book Design: Mary Elizabeth Chupp
Printed by: Carlisle Printing

Carlisle Press
WALNUT CREEK

800.852.4482
2673 Township Road 421
Sugarcreek, OH 44681

Dedicated to

our mothers, Miriam and Edith, who patiently taught us to cook,

our husbands, Josh and Aaron, who gratefully eat what we cook, and

the exceptional cooks in our community, and their generous hospitality.

Table of Contents

Introduction

mily (my sister-in-law) and I decided recently that the wonderful cooks in this community needed to have their recipes used and remembered by others as well. Hence this cookbook. In our community, it's a common practice to invite others for dinner—to return a favor, for a special occasion or holiday, maybe just for the fellowship. Whatever the reason, it's always a fun time, and the food is always great.

I remember one time especially because it captured so well the spirit of hospitality and love. It was my birthday, and my friend Amy invited Josh and me and another couple to their house. The food was, of course, delicious (grilled elk steaks that you could cut with your fork) but what I remember most was that when we got there, her husband told us that we have to realize how special we are—Amy got out her gold silverware for us. It was a small thing, probably the least of her labors that day, but it meant she wanted us there.

I started liking cookbooks about the time I got married. Before, single and working for my Dad (a publisher of many cookbooks, including this one), I often scoffed at the amount of cookbooks married women had. Sensibly, I decided that when *I* got married, I would use only one or two. That was not a resolution that lasted, and today I have many cookbooks and—more remarkable—actually use all of them!

Liking cookbooks is not just about what's for supper, although I've definitely done the "on the couch at four-thirty with three cookbooks" thing. Besides the recipes, they're just fun to read, and if they have photos, fun to look at. Maybe they're compiled by someone you know. Long ago my Mom submitted recipes to a cookbook I now own. I like to use her recipes and think of her, a young-married woman like me— tasting, smelling, and serving the same recipes.

Some people, however, collect cookbooks just for the sake of collecting. While I'm not there yet, I won't laugh at the idea.

For whatever reason you bought this cookbook (or had it given to you)—welcome! Emily and I hope you like it. Read it, use it, mark up the recipes, serve them to your family, or just put it on the shelf with all your other cookbooks. Sharing food, breaking bread, and eating together are magical ways to show love and create bonds among family, friends, and strangers. So go for it! If you don't know what to cook, we've got a few ideas...

Amy Engbretson

We want to thank all the dear sisters who have taken the time to share some of their favorite recipes. Hopefully you will all enjoy making some new tasty dishes for your family.

I am blessed to be the wife of a wonderful man, Aaron Troyer (son of Orlie and Mary Troyer), and the mother of a sweet two-year-old girl, Janice Faith. We are also anticipating the birth of another blessing from God in April.

Aaron works at Foothill Post and Lumber with his dad and brothers. We own 20 acres, and built a little house on it the summer before we were married. Our home is located close to the mountains, and we love to take hikes whenever we have the time.

Amy and I have enjoyed compiling this cookbook, and we wish you all many happy hours cooking, and the Lord's blessings.

Emily Troyer

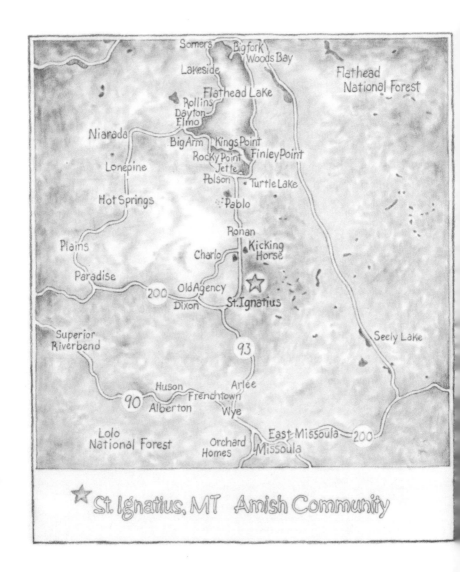

The Pioneers of the St. Ignatius Amish Community

We moved to the Mission Valley from Rexford, Montana in 1997. We were the only Amish family and worked for Frank Pope, a local rancher, from February to September until Orlie Troyers came. We have six children: Heidi (14), Emily (11), Rebekah (8), Michael (6), Katrina (3), and Kristi (1½). Leroy has a butcher shop, which is seasonal, so we raise produce in the summer, as well as butchering chickens.

Leroy and Laura Miller

~

My name is Mary Lynn (Miller) Troyer, and my husband is Orlie Troyer. I moved to Rexford, Montana, in 1975 with my parents, when I was 13 years old. We have lived in Montana ever since, except for a 1½ year stay in Michigan. Orlie and I met in Rexford and were married there in 1980. Three sons were born to us there: Aaron in '83, Abie in '85, and Matthew in '89. In 1991 while living in Michigan, our only daughter, Bethany, was born. After moving back to Rexford, Caleb was added to our family in 1995. In the fall of '97, we moved to St. Ignatius, Montana. Micah was born in 1998, the first Amish baby to be born here.

We own a sawmill and a post and pole business where all our sons are employed. Our oldest son Aaron is married to Emily Engbretson, and they have one daughter, Janice Faith. We all love the mountains, and a highlight of the summer is spending a week in the Montana wilderness. We pack all our supplies in on horses, fishing the creeks and rivers, hiking, and just enjoying God's great outdoors. Every fall we all go on a week-long hunting trip. All of the children, including Bethany, are good woodsmen and hunters, and we usually come home with a winter's supply of meat. We prefer elk meat and I usually fix it same as beef, except for a few special recipes.

Orlie and Mary Troyer

~

We moved to St. Ignatius from Rexford with our five children in the fall of 1997. We were the third family arriving and we rented the place, where Simon Millers now live, from George Biggs. John is the son of John A. and Kathryn Miller, and I am the daughter of Dave and Verna Miller. Our first job was helping Leroy build a basement home for $6.00 an hour. We then decided to start a mini barn business. Our first barn took 13 days to build. Today such a barn takes one day!

We have had ups and downs in the growing years we have been here, but in looking back we can clearly see God's leading hand. Therefore we press on toward the mark of our high calling in Christ Jesus.

John and Ruby Miller

Ray Miller

View of the Mission Valley with the Mission Mountains in the background.

About St. Ignatius and the Mission Valley

The Mission Valley lies from north to south along the western front of the Mission Mountains. Flathead Lake forms the northern boundary, the Missions stand to the east, and the south and west edges rise into low, rolling mountains.

From above, the valley is a 15x30-mile checkerboard of all shades of greens and yellow. Timber in the valley follows the winding course of Mission and Post Creeks. Older homesteads are usually shaded by maples and fruit trees, but the valley is primarily agricultural—open hay and grazing land.

The valley lies at 3500 feet, allowing us good gardens most years, and only barely ripe melons and tomatoes in cooler years. Spring is cool and rainy, summers dry and clear, fall some of both, and winter fluctuates wildly, from a week of clear -20° days to 35° and dense fog.

Hay, pastures, lawns and gardens are irrigated from a canal that parallels the base of the mountains, catching summer snow melt. Twelve inch underground main lines carry water down into the valley where we irrigate with either hand or wheel lines. Irrigation begins after first cutting hay and continues into September.

From where we live, on clear days parts of the Mission, Swan, Rattlesnake, and Reservation Divide mountain ranges are visible. The highest peaks in the Missions are just under 10,000 feet, and retain some snow all summer.

Valley History

The first white person in the Mission Valley was David Thompson, sent by the Northwest Fur Company to establish trade with the natives. After building a trading post near present-day Thompson Falls, he traveled from camp to camp trading beads, jewelry, tobacco, and other merchandise for furs. On a trip to the main Flathead camp at what is now Dixon, Montana, southwest of our community, he was told of Flathead Lake, expressed interest in seeing the lake, and on March 1, 1812, he and his Indian guides traveled north to a hill overlooking the lake, and the Mission Valley to the south. David Thompson returned to his posts farther west, and not until 33 years later the first permanent settlement was established at Fort Connah, six miles north of St. Ignatius. In 1854 the Catholic Mission in St. Ignatius was founded, and by the mid 1850s over a thousand Flathead, Kalispell, and Pend d' Oreille Indians settled around the Mission, planting crops and attending the Mission schools.

Fort Connah, built in 1846, stands as a sentinel of the Mission Valley's colorful past.

Fort Connah

North of the community along timbered Post Creek stands an old weathered log storehouse, possibly the oldest structure in Montana. The storehouse, part of Hudson's Bay trading post, was built in 1846, and served as an important trading center for the Kootenai, Pend', Oreille, and Salish tribes. This post supplied Mission Valley natives with guns, axes, traps, beads, mirrors, and many other items in exchange for buffalo, elk, and beaver hides. For 25 years, this little outpost was witness to strings of packhorses, loaded with hides and meat, snaking out of sight to the west, bands of Indians setting up their buffalo hide lodges along the creek, and the bearded, buck-skin clad trappers and their families. Today, the little log building stands alone, a link to the colorful past of the Mission Valley.

Wildlife

Out in the valley, the most easily seen wildlife is, of course, the universal and adaptable whitetail, along with an occasional coyote or red fox. The absence of timber or brushy cover in most of the valley restricts larger game to the timber at the base of the mountain. A good spotting scope is essential here. From our front lawn we see whitetail, mule deer, elk, mountain goat, grizzly and black bear, mountain lion, bobcat, coyote, and fox.

In early spring, the elk herd feeds in the greening hay fields, and as summer progresses they move to higher elevations, where we see them in the mountain meadows. The goats are always on the high rocky peaks and mountain faces. Through a spotting scope we can watch them pick their way across the rocks. Lions and bobcats are seen only rarely. In the winter, bears are in their dens, but throughout the spring and summer, we see many black bears. Grizzlies generally stay at higher elevations, but it takes only the scent of a dead cow or ripening sweet corn to bring them down into the valley at night. Goats, sheep, chickens, fruit, and sweet corn are irresistible to a grizzly, and many of us have discovered by daylight the aftermath of a grizzly raid—broken fruit trees, flattened corn, demolished chicken houses, and occasionally a dead sheep or goat. Some of our wildlife can be frightening, but mostly we enjoy the sightings and presence of the animal world around us.

The Reservation

Isaac Ingalls Stevens became the first Governor of the newly created Washington Territory, which included western Montana, and entered the region in 1853. After considerable effort a conference was arranged at Council Grove, near what is now Missoula, Montana, attended by Governor Stevens, several officials from the Indian department, Father Hoecken, and three Indian chiefs: Victor of the Salish tribe, Alexander of the Kalispell, and Michelle of the Kootenai. Many meetings later, an agreement was drawn up designating an area eighty miles long by forty miles wide, covering 1,243,969 acres, for the exclusive use of the three tribes. An Indian Agency was established in the Jocko area, and farm machinery, stock, and seeds were distributed.

By 1871, 105 farms were reported under cultivation. In 1910 Congress passed a bill authorizing a survey to be made of the reservation, and allotments to be made to the Indians, with the surplus to be sold to homesteaders. Each tribal member was allotted acreage they selected, and applications for homesteads were taken for the surplus land. By the winter of 1910, the Mission Valley was settled in a patchwork pattern of tribal and private lands. Today we own private property within the reservation. The tribes own much of the forests on the reservation, and manage the hunting, fishing, recreational opportunities, and resources.

The Mission

The fur trading companies, expanding westward, sent Iroquois parties to the peaceful Flathead tribes to teach them the ways and means of fur trapping. They told stories of the white medicine man, the Black Robes (Jesuit priests of the Catholic Missions in the east) who could work Big Medicine. Thinking of their enemies, the Blackfeet, the Flatheads imagined using the Big Medicine of the Black Robes against the powerful Blackfeet. In 1831 four Flatheads made the long journey to St. Louis, Missouri, in search of the Black Robes. Even with the help of Governor Clark, they were unable to find a Black Robe to return with them. None of the four disappointed Indians made it home alive.

In 1835 the Flatheads again sent a party of three men to Missouri. They contacted the Black Robes who promised to send a father as soon as they could spare one. Over a year passed, with no sign of any white man, so a third party—two Flatheads and one Nez Perce, set out for St. Louis. While traveling through Sioux territory, they encountered a war party and were killed. The Indian tribe remained resolute, and at the next council, two men volunteered to try again. Finally in 1840, Father Pierre Jean Desmet was met at Green River, Wyoming, by the Flatheads, and escorted to Montana. He baptized 200 children and 50 adults before returning to Missouri, promising to bring more missionaries the following year. The next spring Father Desmet, two priests, and three laymen, with four two-wheeled carts and one wagon loaded with axes, an alter, books, and even an organ made their way west. After near starvation, they established a Mission in the Bitterroot Valley, 100 miles south of the Mission Valley. After 13 years and the establishment of a mission on the Idaho-Washington line that was unsuccessful due to flooding, the Flatheads told the father of a place to the east called the Rendezvous, considered common ground to the surrounding tribes. The fathers visited the site, and found good water, soil, grass, and timber. On September 24, 1854, the St. Ignatius Mission was established.

In the following years, the Mission grew into a large cultural and spiritual presence in western Montana. Barns, schools, saw mills, and a flour mill were built, with over 1000 Indians calling it home. In 1891 the large brick church was built, which today is an important historical landmark, and a still-functioning part of the valley's history.

Breads

Notes

100% Whole Wheat Bread

Amy Engbretson

4 c. warm water
¾ c. olive oil
½ c. honey
3 Tbsp. instant yeast
3 Tbsp. wheat gluten
2 Tbsp. lecithin granules
1 Tbsp. sea salt
11-12 c. ground Prairie Gold flour

Mix first three ingredients in a mixer. Add yeast, gluten, lecithin, salt, and 4 cups flour. Mix well. Add 6 cups flour and mix well. Continue adding flour by ½ cups until dough scrapes side of mixer clean. Mix on low for 10 minutes. Let set for five minutes. Divide into 1½ pound loaves (depending on your pan size). Roll out and form loaves, place in greased bread pans, and prick with fork. Let rise for 30 minutes. Bake at 300° for 30-35 minutes (increase oven temperature in altitudes above 3000° feet). Remove from oven, let cool for five minutes before taking out of pans. Cool on wire racks. Yield: five loaves.

Whole Wheat Bread

Mrs. Jeremy (Rose) Miller

Six Loaves:

4½ c. warm water
1¾ c. olive or vegetable oil
1 c. honey
3 eggs
1 Tbsp. salt
2 Tbsp. lecithin, optional
⅓ c. instant yeast
whole wheat flour

Four Loaves:	Two Loaves
3 c. –	1½ c. warm water
1¼ c. –	½-⅔ c. olive or vegetable oil
⅔ c. –	⅓ c. honey
2 –	1 egg(s)
2 tsp. –	1 tsp. salt
4 tsp. –	2 tsp. lecithin, optional
¼ c. –	2 Tbsp. instant yeast
	whole wheat flour

Mix first seven ingredients plus some flour in a Bosch mixer. Add remaining flour, several cups at a time, beating well after each addition. I use Bronze Chief Montana Wheat flour. Dough should be sticky. Cover and let rise for 15 minutes. Punch down and let rise another 10 minutes. Put in pans and let rise for approx. 25 minutes. Bake at 350° until lightly browned, then reduce heat to 275°. Should bake approx. 1 hour total. Delicious!

Ruby's 100% Whole Wheat Bread
Ruby Miller

4½ c. warm water
2 c. vegetable oil
1¼ c. honey
1 Tbsp. salt
3 eggs
3½ tsp. wheat gluten
2 tsp. lecithin
⅓ c. yeast, scant
Hi-Gluten Bronze Chief flour

Mix first seven ingredients. When honey is dissolved, add yeast and let set until bubbly, approx. 10 minutes. Add flour until right consistency, approx. 12 cups. Knead well (mixer works great). Let rise for 30 minutes, punch down, and let rise another 30 minutes or until almost double in size. Divide into pans, making seven 1¼ lb. loaves. Don't let rise too high when in pans as they rise in oven. Delicious, soft, and healthy bread.

Italian Garlic Bread
Amy Engbretson

3 Tbsp. instant yeast
3 c. warm water
3 Tbsp. olive oil
3 Tbsp. sugar
1 Tbsp. salt
1 egg
8-9 c. all-purpose flour
 Herb Garlic Butter:
1 c. butter, softened
2½ tsp. garlic powder
1 Tbsp. Italian seasoning
1 Tbsp. parsley
2 tsp. oregano
2 Tbsp. Parmesan cheese

Mix yeast and warm water. Add oil, egg, sugar, and salt; mix well. Add flour until desired consistency. Mix well and knead slightly. Quarter dough and roll out on a floured surface. Roll up lengthwise (rolls should be a foot long and 2-3 inches wide). Score each loaf four times, diagonally. Place on two 9x13 pans, two on each. Bake at 325° for 15-20 minutes or until lightly golden. Do not overbake. Let cool, then slice and spread garlic butter on both sides of every piece. Brush tops with remaining garlic butter. Wrap loaf in tinfoil and heat at 250° for 10 minutes just before serving. Yield: four loaves, 12 pieces each. If serving crowds, make one loaf for every 10 people.

Raisin Bread
Edith Engbretson

2 Tbsp. yeast
1½ c. warm water
1½ c. boiling water
1½ c. raisins
1 c. oatmeal
½ c. light Karo
2 tsp. salt
2 Tbsp. butter
7½ c. Robin Hood flour

Mix yeast and warm water, set aside. Mix boiling water, raisins, oatmeal, and butter; cool. Add Karo and salt, mix all together. Add flour, let rise, punch down, and put in two loaf pans. Let rise one hour and bake at 350° for 30 minutes. Cool on wire rack. Extremely soft and delicious!

Banana Bread
Edith Engbretson

½ c. shortening or margarine
1 c. sugar
2 eggs
2 c. flour
½ tsp. baking powder
½ tsp. soda
½ tsp. salt
3 bananas, mashed

Cream together shortening or margarine, sugar, and eggs. Add mashed bananas, then dry ingredients. Sprinkle nuts on top if desired. Bake in bread pans. This is a great way to use up overripe bananas.

Blessed are those who give without remembering and receive without forgetting.

Sweet Hawaiian Bread
Mrs. Amy Miller

4-4½ c. all-purpose flour
⅓ c. sugar
1 tsp. salt
2 (.25 oz.) env. active dry yeast
½ c. warm water
½ c. warm milk
¼ c. butter, softened
2 Tbsp. honey
3 lg. eggs, divided

Combine 1½ c. flour, sugar, salt, and yeast in a large bowl; mix well. Add water, milk, butter, and honey. Beat until moistened. Add two eggs and beat until blended. Stir in enough remaining flour until a soft dough forms. Knead dough on a lightly floured surface until smooth and elastic, 8-10 minutes. Place in a greased bowl, cover, and let rise in a warm place until almost double in size (one hour). Grease baking sheet, punch down dough, and shape into a ball. Place on prepared sheet, cover, and let rise until almost double in size, 30-40 minutes. Preheat oven to 350°. Beat remaining egg and brush onto loaf. Bake until golden, 25-35 minutes. Cool on rack.

Sausage Roll
Mary L. Troyer

1 loaf frozen white bread dough
 (I use my own)
½ lb. sausage, fried
1 c. shredded mozzarella cheese
½ c. bacon, fried, crumbled
1 egg

Roll out bread dough into a 12x5 rectangle. Mix next four ingredients together and spread on dough. Roll up, starting at wide end, and form into a loaf. Place in greased bread pan and brush with melted butter and sprinkle with parsley flakes. Bake immediately at 350° for 25-30 minutes or until nicely browned. Cool completely. Slice into half-inch slices. Top each slice with a slice of tomato and mozzarella cheese. Heat until cheese is melted.

Cornmeal Dinner Rolls

Lydiann Troyer

⅓ c. cornmeal
½ c. white sugar
2 tsp. salt
½ c. vegetable oil
2 c. milk
1 Tbsp. yeast
¼ c. water
2 eggs, beaten
6-7 c. bread flour

Cook first five ingredients till thick. Remove from heat. Cool until lukewarm, then add yeast, water, and eggs. Stir well. Add flour to form a soft dough. Knead in a bowl and cover. Let rise until double and punch down. Roll out to 1 inch thickness and cut with a cookie cutter, or the size you like. Place on greased cookie sheets. Let rise. Bake at 375° for 15 minutes or until golden. Brush with butter.

Easy Rolls

Sheila Schrock

4 c. warm water
½ c. white sugar
¼ c. shortening
4 Tbsp. yeast
2 tsp. salt
1 egg, room temperature
6½ c. flour
6 c. donut mix
 Icing:
powdered sugar
½ c. margarine
1 c. brown sugar
¼ tsp. salt
¼ c. milk

Measure water, sugar, and yeast in bowl, and let set till bubbly. Then add salt, shortening, and egg, stirring until shortening is dissolved. Add flour, then donut mix, and mix only until all flour and donut mix is worked in. Do not knead. Let rise till double, pat down and let rise again. Roll out and spread with cinnamon, brown sugar and butter. Roll up, slice and place in a greased pan. Let rise. Bake at 350° for 20-30 minutes. Ice with brown sugar icing. *Icing:* Stir margarine, salt, and brown sugar over low heat until melted. Add milk and bring to a boil. Cool slightly. Add powdered sugar to desired consistency.

Dinner Rolls
Emily Troyer

1 c. milk
½ c. white sugar
¼ c. butter
2 tsp. salt
1 c. water
2 Tbsp. yeast
2 eggs, beaten
5-5½ c. flour

Scald milk and pour over white sugar, butter and salt. Add water to cool milk to lukewarm. Add yeast and let set for 10 minutes. Add eggs and then flour. Let rise until double in bulk (about 1 hour). Punch down and let rise again. Make balls with dough and put on greased cookie sheet. Let rise 30 minutes. Bake at 350° for 20 minutes or until lightly browned. Serves 30 people.

Parker House Rolls
Amy Engbretson

2½ tsp. dry yeast
1 c. milk
4 Tbsp. unsalted butter, melted
2 Tbsp. white sugar
2 eggs, beaten
4¼ c. bread flour
2 tsp. salt
melted butter to glaze tops

Mix yeast and ½ c. milk in bowl; let stand for 5 minutes, stir to dissolve. Warm remaining milk in saucepan with butter and sugar. Stir till butter melts. Cool till lukewarm, then beat in eggs. Mix flour and salt in bowl, make a well in the center and pour in yeast and butter mixture. Mix to form soft, sticky dough. Knead on floured surface until smooth and elastic. Dough should be soft, not dry. Let rise 1½ hours, then punch down and let rest 10 minutes. Form into rolls and put on greased baking sheet; let rise 30 minutes or till doubled in size. Bake at 425° for 15-20 minutes. Do not overbake. Cool on rack and brush with melted butter. Serves 16 people.

Cinnamon Rolls
Laura Ann Miller

7 c. water
1 c. margarine
1½ c. sugar
6 eggs
1 Tbsp. salt
8 c. donut mix
5 Tbsp. yeast
12 c. flour
3 c. flour
 Sour Cream Caramel Icing:
¼ c. butter
½ c. sour cream
¾ c. brown sugar
 Caramel Icing:
½ c. butter
1 c. brown sugar
¼ c. rich milk or cream
1 tsp. vanilla
2 c. powdered sugar

Mix first eight ingredients together, then add approx. 3 more cups of flour. Let rise till double. Roll out and spread with butter, brown sugar and cinnamon. Roll up, starting at wide end. Cut approx. 1 inch and place in pans. Let rise 15 minutes. Bake at 350° for approx. 20 minutes. *For Sour Cream Caramel Icing:* Melt together, but do not boil. Delicious poured over warm cinnamon rolls! *For Caramel Icing:* Melt butter, add brown sugar. Cook over low heat, stirring constantly, for 3-4 minutes. Add milk and stir till mixture boils again. Remove from heat. Add vanilla. Cool. Add powdered sugar, stirring very well.

Butterhorns
Emily Troyer

1 Tbsp. yeast with 1 tsp. sugar
1 c. water
½ tsp. salt
½ c. sugar
½ c. butter, melted
3 eggs, beaten
4½ c. flour

Mix dough and let rise for an hour. Roll out dough and cut into triangles. Roll triangles to form a butterhorn and put on greased pans. Let rise and bake at 350° for 30 minutes or until lightly brown.

Deluxe Breadsticks

Rachel Troyer

1½ c. lukewarm water
1 Tbsp. yeast
1 Tbsp. white sugar
2 Tbsp. vegetable oil
1 Tbsp. salt
½ c. spelt bran, optional
1 c. wheat flour
3½ c. bread flour
  Herb Mixture:
2 Tbsp. Parmesan cheese
½ c. Italian dressing
1 tsp. garlic powder
1 Tbsp. Italian seasoning
½ Tbsp. oregano

Mix first five ingredients well. Add bran and flour. Knead as for bread. Spread on a 12x17 cookie sheet. Spread herb mixture over dough and let rise until double. Bake at 350° for 21 minutes. Top with pepperoni and grated mozzarella cheese. Return to oven until cheese is melted.

Parmesan Breadsticks

Edith Engbretson

1 Tbsp. yeast
1½ c. warm water
2 Tbsp. sugar
¾ c. butter, divided
½ tsp. salt
4½ c. flour
garlic salt
Parmesan cheese
warm pizza sauce

Dissolve yeast in warm water. Add sugar; let set 5 minutes. Add ½ c. butter (melted), salt, and flour. Cover and let rise until double. Roll out into a rectangle. Cut dough into strips. Twist each and place on a greased cookie sheet. Brush with remaining butter and sprinkle with garlic salt and Parmesan cheese. Let rise. Bake at 350° for 20 minutes. Dip in warm pizza sauce.

Italian Breadsticks

Amy Engbretson

1 Tbsp. yeast
1 c. warm water
1 tsp. sugar
1 Tbsp. olive oil
1 tsp. salt
2½-3 c. Softex flour
⅓ c. Italian dressing
¼ tsp. garlic powder
¼ tsp. oregano
¼ tsp. thyme
dash pepper
1 c. shredded mozzarella cheese
¼ c. Parmesan cheese

Mix first three ingredients, let set 5 minutes. Add olive oil, salt, and flour; knead till smooth. Let rise 40 minutes. Punch down and let stand 5 minutes. Press into 14 inch pizza pan and spread with remaining ingredients, in order given. Bake at 450° for 15-20 minutes. Cut into strips and serve. Delicious! Serves 7 people.

Garlic Parmesan Breadsticks

Mrs. Marty (Esther) Miller

1 Tbsp. yeast
1½ c. warm water
2 Tbsp. white sugar
½ c. butter, melted
½ tsp. salt
4½ c. bread flour
garlic salt
Parmesan cheese

Mix warm water, yeast, and sugar. Let set 5 minutes. Add salt, melted butter, and flour. Knead 5 minutes. Let it rise for 30 minutes. Roll out in a 10x24 rectangle. Cut in 5x1 inch strips. Twist and place on a greased cookie sheet. Melt ¼ c. butter and brush over breadsticks. Sprinkle with garlic salt and Parmesan cheese. Let rise and bake at 350° for 20 minutes.

Cornbread

Mrs. Steve (Linda) Kauffman

2 c. cornmeal
2 c. brown flour (or white)
¾ c. brown sugar
2 tsp. soda
½ c. butter
2 eggs

Add enough cream and milk to make a very stiff dough. Bake at 400° for 15-20 minutes. For our family I make a single batch, then put it in a buttered pie pan. Eat with tomato soup or with jelly or apple butter.

Golden Cornbread

Esther Yoder

2 eggs
½ c. sugar
½ c. butter
1 c. cornmeal
1 c. flour
1 tsp. baking powder
1 tsp. baking soda
½ tsp. salt
1 c. buttermilk

Beat eggs and sugar; add melted butter. Alternately add dry ingredients and buttermilk. Transfer to 9x13 pan. Bake at 375° until golden brown. Serve with chili or bean soup.

Herb Pizza Crust

Amy Engbretson

1 Tbsp. honey
1 Tbsp. oregano
½ Tbsp. garlic powder
1 c. warm water
1 egg
1 Tbsp. salt
1 Tbsp. basil
1 Tbsp. yeast
2 c. whole wheat flour
½ c. white flour

Mix honey, water, and yeast. Let set 10 minutes until bubbly. Mix in egg and seasonings, then add flour gradually until a smooth, elastic ball of dough is formed. Knead on floured surface a few minutes. Roll onto cookie sheet. Prebake 10 minutes at 350° before putting on toppings.

Pizza Dough

Arlene Bontrager

2 Tbsp. yeast
3 Tbsp. sugar
2⅔ c. warm water
¼ tsp. garlic powder
3 Tbsp. vegetable oil
1 Tbsp. salt
½ tsp. oregano
6¼ c. flour, maybe not quite as much

Prebake at 400° for 10-15 minutes. Take out of oven and add your favorite toppings. Bake at 350° till done.

Garlic Toast
Julie Hochstetler

bread
butter
garlic salt
garlic powder
oregano

Spread one side of a slice of bread with butter. Sprinkle with garlic salt, garlic powder, and oregano. Toast on griddle. Try using hot dog buns. Great with spaghetti.

Favorite Biscuits
Fannie Yoder

2 c. flour
4 tsp. baking powder
½ tsp. cream of tartar
1 tsp. salt
½ c. shortening
1 egg
½ c. milk

Mix flour, baking powder, cream of tartar, and salt. Blend in shortening, egg, and milk. Bake at 400° for 20 minutes or until golden brown.

Buttermilk Biscuits (for deep frying)
Dena Hostetler

7 c. bread flour
⅓ c. baking powder
1 Tbsp. salt
1 Tbsp. cream of tartar
¼ c. sugar
1 c. margarine
2 c. buttermilk

Mix all ingredients together. Whole milk works as well as buttermilk, add more milk if dough is too stiff. Divide into golf ball size balls. Roll out and put your favorite pie filling in, wash around edge of dough and fold in half and press ends together well. Deep fry at 350°. Serves 35 people.

Creamy Chive Ring

Sheila Schrock

1 Tbsp. yeast
¼ c. water
1 c. milk
6 Tbsp. butter
¼ tsp. salt
¼ c. instant potato flakes
⅓ c. white sugar
1 egg
3¾-4¼ c. flour
Filling:
1 egg
¾ c. evaporated milk
1 c. chives, chopped
½ tsp. salt

Heat milk, butter, salt, potato flakes, and sugar until butter is melted, stirring continually. Cool slightly. Dissolve yeast in water in a large bowl. Add milk mixture, egg, and flour. Mix well. Cover and let rise. Divide dough in two. Roll out in rectangular shape. Spread with the filling. Roll up and pinch seam closed. Place in a greased pie plate, seam side down, in a ring. Take scissors and cut from the top down almost all the way through. Rings will stay upright but lay at a slant against each other. Brush beaten egg on top, sprinkle with sesame seeds. Let rise and bake at 350°. Optional: Roll dough in 2 circles, spread with filling. Cut into wedges and roll as butterhorns. *Filling:* Heat and stir to almost boiling. Cool and let set till thick.

"Invention is 10% inspiration and 90% perspiration."
Thomas Edison

Kolaches
Brenda Beachy

1 c. margarine, melted
½ c. sugar
2 c. milk, scalded,
    that has been cooled
2 tsp. salt
½ c. warm water
6 egg yolks
6 c. flour
  Butter Cream Frosting:
¼ c. butter
2 tsp. vanilla
3 c. powdered sugar
½ tsp. salt
¼ c. milk

Mix first five ingredients together, then whisk in egg yolks with wire whip. Add flour. Mix well and set in warm place. Let rise until double in size. Roll ½" thick and cut with mandarin can or donut cutter. Brush with melted butter. Let rise till double. Make indentation with a small bottle or container. Fill with fruit filling of your choice. Let rise a little, then bake at 350° till bottoms are lightly brown. Cool then ice. *Butter Cream Frosting:* Combine butter, salt, vanilla, and 1 c. powdered sugar. Add milk and remaining sugar. Mix till smooth and creamy. Add more sugar or milk to right spreading consistency. Yield: 32 Kolaches

Baked Doughnuts
Sarah Ann Miller

2 c. warm water
1 Tbsp. yeast
3 Tbsp. sugar
3 c. donut mix
2 c. flour
  Filling:
2 boxes instant vanilla pudding
3 c. milk
8 oz. cream cheese

Mix yeast, sugar, and water and stir well. Add donut mix and flour, mix thoroughly. Cover and let rise for a while. Roll out ½ inch thick. Cut with cookie cutter or can ring. Let rise a while again. Bake at 350° for 20 minutes or until golden. Cut in half when cool, but not all the way. *Filling:* Beat pudding and milk accordingly. In a separate bowl beat cream cheese till smooth. Beat in pudding a little at a time. Fill split donuts and put a glaze on top.

Ways to Go Green

Buy plain white toilet paper, tissues, and paper towels

Reuse grocery bags

Turn off lights as much as possible

Plant trees

Avoid keeping fridge and freezer too cold - the temperature for refrigerator should be 38°F and freezer 5°F

Water lawns at night to eliminate evaporation

Use cold water rather than hot whenever possible

Turn water heater to 121°F

Limit your use of disposable items

Pour boiling water down drain once a week to melt fat that may be building up

Use cloth diapers

Substitutes

For bread crumbs use crushed corn or wheat flakes or other dry cereal.

For butter use ⅞ cup solid shortening plus ½ tsp. salt.

For buttermilk use 1 Tbsp. lemon juice or vinegar, and enough fresh milk to make 1 cup; let it set 5 minutes before using.

1 med. onion - 2 Tbsp. instant minced onion or 1 tsp. onion powder

1 garlic clove - ⅛ tsp. garlic powder or ¼ tsp. garlic salt

1 Tbsp. fresh herbs - 1 tsp. dried herbs

Spices

allspice - cakes, cookies, pies, breads, pickles, relishes

basil - tomatoes, barbecue sauce, salads, chicken, tomato sauce

celery seed - meatloaf, beef, vegetable stews, bean salad

cloves - ham, beets, hot spiced beverages, cakes, pies

Breakfast Foods

Notes

Morning Mix-Up

Julie Hochstetler

2 c. hash browns
1 c. chopped fully cooked ham
½ c. chopped onions
2 Tbsp. cooking oil
6 eggs
salt and pepper
1 c. shredded cheese
minced fresh chives

In skillet sauté potatoes, ham, and onion in cooking oil until potatoes are done. Beat eggs, salt, and pepper; add to the skillet. Cook, stirring occasionally, until eggs are set. Remove from heat and stir in cheese. Spoon onto serving platter. Sprinkle with chives. Serve with juice and toast. Might be able to use this for a camping recipe. Serves 4 people.

Breakfast Casserole

Rachel Troyer

2 c. sausage, browned
2 c. ham, diced
1 c. smoky links, sliced
1 c. bacon, fried and cut up
1½ doz. eggs, scrambled
cheese slices
2 lb. Tater Tots
2 (10¾ oz.) cans cream of chicken
   soup
1 (16 oz.) cont. sour cream
   Cornflake Mixture:
2 c. cornflakes, slightly crushed
½ c. butter

Mix together cream of chicken and sour cream. Set aside. Layer ingredients in a large casserole dish in order given. Bake at 350° for approx. 1 hour. Top with cheese. Enjoy!

Campers' Omelette
Lorene Yoder

½ lb. sliced bacon
2 med. potatoes,
   unpeeled and diced
1 med. onion, chopped
½ green bell pepper, diced
6 lg. eggs, beaten fluffy with whisk
salt and pepper to taste
2 Roma tomatoes, sliced
8 oz. shredded cheddar cheese

Fry bacon crisp, crumble for later use. Fry diced potatoes in bacon fat until tender and lightly browned. Add onion and bell pepper, stirring occasionally till onion is cooked. Reduce heat. Season beaten eggs with salt and pepper. Keep in mind that cheese and bacon are salty. Add eggs, stir cook 2 or 3 minutes till eggs are set. Sprinkle cheese and bacon over eggs and arrange tomato slices on top. Cover skillet until cheese melts. Cut into wedges and serve hot. Serves 4 to 6 people.

Gold Rush Brunch
Faith Ann Yoder

5 lg. potatoes
onion, optional
2 Tbsp. parsley
1 lb. ham, bacon, or sausage
10 eggs, scrambled
  White Sauce:
1 c. sour cream
¼ c. flour
¼ c. butter, melted
¼ tsp. salt
1¾ c. milk
pepper to taste

Shred the potatoes, fry in butter with onions and 2 Tbsp. parsley. When potatoes are tender put in greased 9x13 pan. Add meat and scrambled eggs. Top with the following. *White Sauce:* Melt butter, add sour cream, flour, salt, and pepper. Stir well, then slowly add milk until thick. Take off of heat and add Velveeta cheese. Put on top of potatoes, meat, and eggs. Bake at 400° for 30 minutes.

Whole Wheat Oatmeal Pancakes (The Best)

Mrs. Johnny (Ruby) Miller

2 eggs
1 c. oatmeal
1 c. whole wheat flour
1½ c. milk
4 Tbsp. vegetable oil
2 Tbsp. sugar
6 tsp. baking powder
½ tsp. salt

Beat eggs; add milk, vegetable oil, and sugar. Stir in flour, baking powder, salt, and oats. Let set a few minutes before frying. If mixture thickens too much, add more milk. Family favorite!

Whole Wheat Oatmeal Pancakes

Mrs. Jeremy (Rose) Miller

2 eggs
1½ c. milk
4 Tbsp. olive oil (or vegetable oil)
2 Tbsp. honey (or sugar)
1 c. whole wheat flour
1 c. quick oats
1½ Tbsp. baking powder
½ tsp. salt

Beat eggs until fluffy; add milk, oil, and honey. Stir in flour, oats, baking powder, and salt. Let set a few minutes before frying. If mixture thickens too much, add a little more milk.

Pancakes

Mrs. David (Katie) Kurtz

3 eggs
2 c. milk
1 tsp. salt
2 c. flour
4 tsp. baking powder
4 Tbsp. butter, melted

Put salt, flour, and baking powder in a bowl. Add milk and beat with a whisk. Add eggs and beat again. Add melted butter last. Recipe says "Best Pancakes in the World."

Honey Wheat Pancakes
Esther Yoder

2 c. wheat flour
2 Tbsp. honey
4 tsp. baking powder
1 tsp. salt
¼ c. butter, melted
2 eggs, separated
1¾ c. milk

Beat egg yolks; add butter, honey, and milk, followed by dry ingredients; mix well, then fold in stiffly beaten egg whites. Fry on hot griddle. Yield: 6 pancakes or 4 large waffles.

Blueberry French Toast
Mrs. Jeremy (Rose) Miller

12 slices bread
1 (8 oz.) pkg. cream cheese
1 c. fresh or frozen blueberries
12 eggs
2 c. milk
⅓ c. maple syrup or honey
 Sauce:
1 c. sugar
2 Tbsp. cornstarch
1 c. water
1 c. fresh or frozen blueberries
1 Tbsp. butter

Cut bread into 1 inch cubes; place half in a greased 13x9x2 baking dish. Cut cream cheese into small pieces; place over bread. Top with blueberries and remaining bread. In a large bowl, beat eggs. Add milk and syrup; mix well. Pour over bread mixture. Cover and chill for 8 hours or overnight. Remove from refrigerator 30 minutes before baking. Cover and bake at 350° for 30 minutes. Uncover; bake 25-30 minutes more or until golden brown and the center is set. In a saucepan, combine sugar and cornstarch; add water. Bring to a boil over medium heat. Boil for 3 minutes, stirring constantly. Stir in blueberries; reduce heat. Simmer for 8-10 minutes or until berries have burst. Stir in butter until melted. Serve hot over French toast. To make huckleberry French toast, use huckleberries instead of blueberries. Serves 6 to 8 people.

Stuffed French Toast
Sheila Schrock

8-10 slices bread
1 (8 oz.) pkg. cream cheese
¼ c. white sugar
4 eggs, beaten
1 c. milk
2 tsp. vanilla
¼ c. white sugar
½ tsp. salt
1 c. pie filling,
    blueberry, strawberry, etc.

Mix cream cheese and white sugar and spread on slices of bread. Cut pieces in half and spread with 1 Tbsp. of pie filling. Put 2 slices together to make a sandwich. Mix remaining ingredients. Dip sandwiches into egg mixture and brown on both sides over medium heat on a buttered griddle. Sprinkle with powdered sugar. Serve immediately with syrup. Serves 8 people.

Apple-Stuffed French Toast
Mrs. Jerry Miller

1 c. brown sugar, packed
½ c. butter, cubed
2 Tbsp. light corn syrup
1 c. chopped pecans
12 slices Italian bread (½" thick)
2 lg. tart apples,
    peeled and thinly sliced
6 eggs
1½ c. milk
1½ tsp. ground cinnamon
1 tsp. vanilla extract
¼ tsp. salt
¼ tsp. ground nutmeg
Caramel Sauce:
½ c. brown sugar, packed
¼ c. butter, cubed
1 Tbsp. light corn syrup

In a small saucepan, combine the brown sugar, butter, and corn syrup; cook and stir over medium heat until thickened. Pour into a greased 13x9x2 baking dish; top with half of the pecans, a single layer of bread and remaining pecans. Arrange apples and remaining bread over the top. In a large bowl, whisk the eggs, milk, cinnamon, vanilla, salt, and nutmeg. Pour over the bread. Cover and refrigerate overnight. Remove from the refrigerator 30 minutes before baking. Bake, uncovered, at 350° for 35-40 minutes or until lightly browned. In a small saucepan combine the sauce ingredients. Cook and stir over medium heat until thickened. Serve with French toast.

Apple Waffles
Amy Engbretson

2 eggs, separated
6 Tbsp. shortening
1 Tbsp. sugar
½ tsp. cinnamon
¼ tsp. salt
2 tsp. baking powder
1 c. milk
1¼ c. flour
1¾ c. grated apples

Beat egg whites. Mix egg yolks, shortening, and sugar. Add to the rest of ingredients. Add egg whites last. Bake in hot waffle iron. These are easy to freeze. When ready to thaw put in oven at 350° for 20 minutes or till hot. Serves 8 people.

Waffles
Sarah Ann Miller

3 c. sifted flour
5 tsp. baking powder
1 tsp. salt
2 tsp. sugar
⅔ c. butter, melted
2 c. milk
4 eggs, separated

Beat egg yolks; add milk; beat again. Add sifted dry ingredients and beat. Add melted butter and beat again. Fold in stiffly beaten egg whites. Bake in preheated, oiled waffle iron until browned. Serve with syrup, fruit topping, and if served for dessert add ice cream.

Elderberry Syrup
Lorene Yoder

4 c. prepared elderberry juice
½ pkg. pectin (Sure-Jell)
3 Tbsp. lemon juice
6 c. sugar (I use only 4)

Pick elderberries off stems and put through grape steamer. Mix juice with pectin and lemon juice; heat and add sugar, and bring to full boil. Can like any jam. We use this on waffles and pancakes. Very good. Can be done with chokecherry juice as well. Yield: approx. 6-7 pints.

Raspberry-Lemon Muffins
Amy Engbretson

1½ c. flour
¼ c. white sugar
¼ c. brown sugar, packed
2 tsp. baking powder
¼ tsp. salt
1 tsp. cinnamon
1 egg, lightly beaten
½ c. butter, melted
½ c. milk
1¼ c. red raspberries
1 tsp. lemon zest, grated
  Topping:
½ c. shredded coconut
½ c. white sugar
¼ c. flour
1 tsp. cinnamon
2 tsp. lemon zest, grated
4 Tbsp. butter, melted
  Glaze:
½ c. powdered sugar
1 Tbsp. fresh lemon juice, strained

Preheat oven to 350°. Prepare muffin cups. Sift together flour, sugars, baking powder, cinnamon, and salt into a large bowl. Make a well in the center. Place egg, melted butter, and milk in the well. Stir with a wooden spoon until ingredients are just mixed; do not overmix. Quickly stir in raspberries and lemon zest. Divide batter among 12 muffin cups. *To Make Topping:* Combine all ingredients except butter into bowl, pour butter over it and stir. Sprinkle evenly over each muffin. Bake muffins 20-25 minutes until nicely browned and firm. Let muffins cool slightly, remove from tins and place on wire rack to cool for 10 minutes. *Glaze:* Combine ingredients till smooth, drizzle over warm muffins. Serves 12 people.

Cinnamon Doughnut Muffins
Brenda Beachy

1¾ c. flour
1½ tsp. baking powder
½ tsp. salt
½ tsp. nutmeg
¼ tsp. cinnamon
¾ c. sugar
⅓ c. vegetable oil
1 egg, lightly beaten
¾ c. milk
jam
  Topping:
¼ c. butter
⅓ c. sugar
1 tsp. cinnamon

In large bowl, combine flour, baking powder, salt, nutmeg, and cinnamon. Combine sugar, vegetable oil, egg, and milk. Stir into dry ingredients just until moistened. Fill paper muffin cups ½ full. Place 1 tsp. jam on top. Cover with batter until ¾ full. Bake at 350° for 20-25 minutes. Immediately dip tops in melted butter then cinnamon-sugar mixture. Optional: Add a dab of soft cream cheese on top of jam.

Golden Harvest Muffins

Amy Engbretson

1 c. all-purpose flour
1 c. whole wheat flour
1 c. sugar
2 tsp. baking soda
1 tsp. cinnamon
½ tsp. salt
¼ tsp. cloves
2 c. shredded apples
½ c. shredded carrots
½ c. coconut
½ c. raisins
½ c. pecans
¾ c. vegetable oil
¼ c. milk
2 tsp. vanilla
2 eggs, beaten

Mix dry ingredients. Add remaining ingredients and stir till just moistened. Line 18 muffin cups with baking cups. Fill ¾ full. Bake at 350° for 20-25 minutes. Serves 18 people.

Sugar-Topped Mocha Cupcakes

Amy Engbretson

2½ c. all-purpose flour
1½ c. plus ⅓ c. sugar, divided
½ c. baking cocoa
2 tsp. baking soda
½ tsp. salt
⅔ c. vegetable oil
2 Tbsp. cider vinegar
1 tsp. vanilla extract
2 c. cold-brewed coffee
½ tsp. cinnamon

In a large mixing bowl, combine the flour, 1½ c. sugar, cocoa, baking soda, and salt. Add the vegetable oil, vinegar, and vanilla. Beat on low speed until blended. Add the coffee; beat on medium speed for two minutes. Fill paper-lined muffin cups ⅔ full. Combine cinnamon and remaining sugar; sprinkle half of the mixture over batter. Bake at 350° for 20-25 minutes or until a toothpick comes out clean. Immediately sprinkle remaining cinnamon sugar over cupcakes. Cool for 10 minutes before removing from pans to wire racks to cool completely . Yield: about 2½ dozen. Serves 30 people.

Granola
Lydiann Troyer

10 c. quick oats
3 pkg. graham crackers,
   coarsely crushed
1 tsp. soda
½ tsp. salt
2 c. vegetable oil or butter
⅔ c. honey
1 lb. pkg. sandwich cookies,
   coarsely crushed

Mix all dry ingredients together. Mix liquid ingredients together, then pour over dry ingredients. Mix well. Bake at 200° for 1¼ hours. Stir every 30 minutes.

Granola
Emily Troyer

10 c. oatmeal
2 c. wheat germ
2 c. coconut
1½ c. brown sugar
½ c. vegetable oil
½ c. honey
2 tsp. vanilla
1 tsp. salt
½ c. peanut butter

Melt vegetable oil, peanut butter, and honey in a small saucepan. Mix rest of ingredients and add oil mixture. Spread on cookie sheets and toast until lightly browned.

Chocolate Chip Granola Cereal
Amy Engbretson

6 c. quick oats
2 c. brown sugar
2 tsp. salt
4 c. whole wheat flour
1 c. toasted coconut
1½ tsp. baking soda
1½ c. butter, melted
1 c. chocolate chips

Mix dry ingredients, except chocolate chips. Add butter and mix well with hands. Put in two cake pans or one large pan. Bake at 380°-400° for 30 minutes. Stir every 10 minutes. Put chips on top when out of oven. Let set 10 minutes, then stir.

Favorite Granola

Mrs. Marty (Esther) Miller

1¼ c. brown sugar
8 c. oatmeal
4 c. whole wheat flour
4 c. coconut
1 pkg. graham crackers,
  coarsely crushed
1 tsp. salt
2 tsp. soda
2 c. butter, melted
chocolate chips, optional

Mix all ingredients together except chocolate chips. Spread on cookie sheets and bake at 250° for 45 minutes, stirring every 15 minutes. After it is slightly cooled you may add chocolate chips if desired.

Granola Cereal

Ella Yutzy

10 c. quick oats
2 pkg. graham crackers,
  coarsely crushed
1½ c. brown sugar
2 c. coconut
2 tsp. soda
1 tsp. salt
1½ c. flax seed
1 c. slivered almonds
2 c. butter or margarine, melted

Mix first eight ingredients, then add melted butter. Put on cookie sheets and toast in 200°-250° oven until dry. Stir occasionally.

Sin causes the cup of joy to spring a leak.

Appetizers and Dips

Notes

Tiny Cherry Cheesecakes

Mrs. Jerry Miller

1 c. all-purpose flour
⅓ c. sugar
¼ c. baking cocoa
½ c. cold butter
2 Tbsp. cold water
 Filling:
1 (8 oz.) pkg. cream cheese
¼ c. sugar
2 Tbsp. milk
1 tsp. vanilla
1 egg
1 (21 oz.) can cherry or
   strawberry pie filling

In a small bowl combine, flour, sugar, and cocoa. Cut in butter until crumbly, gradually add water tossing with a fork until dough forms a ball. Shape into 24 balls. Place in greased miniature muffin cups. Press dough onto the bottom and up the sides of each cup. In a mixing bowl beat cream cheese and sugar until smooth. Beat in milk and vanilla, add egg. Mix thoroughly. Spoon 1 Tbsp. into each cup. Bake at 325° for 15-18 minutes or until set. Cool on wire rack for 30 minutes, then remove from pan. Top with pie filling. Yield: 2 dozen.

Cheese Ball

Amy Engbretson

2 (8 oz.) pkg. cream cheese
2 c. shredded cheddar cheese
1 Tbsp. Worcestershire sauce
½ tsp. garlic salt
1 tsp. onion salt
1 Tbsp. lemon juice
⅛ c. parsley flakes
¼ c. finely chopped nuts

Mix cheeses (potato masher works great), then add rest of ingredients, except for parsley and nuts. Shape into a ball or log and roll in parsley and nuts. Serves 10 people.

Salsa Roll-Ups

Amy Engbretson

6 flour tortillas
1 pt. salsa
1 (8 oz.) pkg. cream cheese,
   softened

Mix cream cheese and salsa and spread on tortillas. Roll up, cut in 1 inch pieces and chill. Serves 6 people.

Mini Pizzas

Mrs. Amy Miller

1 tube pop biscuits
1½ c. cooked chicken cubes
barbecue sauce
bacon
mushrooms
shredded cheese

Grease 10 of a 12 count muffin pan. Press one biscuit into the bottom of each muffin hole for the crusts. Spoon in approx. 1 Tbsp. barbecue sauce in each crust. Top with chicken, bacon, mushrooms, and shredded cheese. Bake at 350° for 15 minutes or until lightly browned. These are also very good with pizza sauce, burger, peppers or whatever pizza toppings you desire.

Chip Dip Casserole

Mrs. Julie Hochstetler

Bottom Layer:
1 (8 oz.) pkg. cream cheese
¼ c. white sugar
1 c. sour cream
¾ c. salad dressing
Second Layer:
1 lb. hamburger, browned
taco seasoning
1 c. salsa

Put lettuce, tomatoes, and cheese on top. Use 9x13 pan.

Salsa Chicken Quesadillas

8 (6") flour tortillas
3 cooked, boneless, skinless chicken
  breast halves, cubed (or canned
  chicken bits)
1 c. shredded cheese
½ c. salsa
½ tsp. chili powder
2 Tbsp. Miracle Whip dressing

Combine salsa, dressing, and chili powder. Spread evenly on bottom half of tortillas, top with chicken and cheese. Fold tortillas in half to enclose filling. Cook in greased skillet over medium heat 4-5 minutes on each side or until both sides are golden brown and cheese is melted. Cut each quesadilla into 3 wedges to serve. Serves 4 people.

Barbecue Beef Taco Plate

Brenda Beachy

2 lb. ground beef
1 env. taco seasoning
½ c. water
2 (8 oz.) pkg. cream cheese, softened
½ c. milk
1 env. Ranch dressing mix
1 chopped green pepper
2 c. shredded lettuce
2 chopped tomatoes
1 bottle honey barbecue sauce
lg. bag tortilla chips

Cook ground beef till done. Drain. Stir in taco seasoning and water. Bring to boil and simmer for 15 minutes. In mixing bowl beat cream cheese, milk, and dressing mix till blended. Spread on 2 (14 inch) plates. Layer beef mixture, lettuce, peppers, cheese, and tomatoes. Drizzle with barbecue sauce. Dip with chips. We like to fix this on individual plates for Saturday evening supper.

Sugared Pretzel and Chex Mix

Mrs. Johnny (Ruby) Miller

¾ c. butter
½ c. brown sugar
1 bag stick pretzels
1 box Corn Chex

Melt butter and sugar. Pour over pretzel and Chex mixture; mix well. Put on cookie sheet and bake for 12 minutes at 325°. Easy and finger-licking good!

Caramel Corn

Edith Engbretson

1½ c. unpopped corn
1 c. butter
2 c. brown sugar
½ c. Karo
1 tsp. soda
1 tsp. vanilla

Pop popcorn first, then cook butter, sugar and Karo together 5 minutes. Add soda and vanilla. Pour over popcorn and stir well.

Rice Krispie Candy

Edith Engbretson

¼ c. butter, melted
4 c. small marshmallows
5 c. Rice Krispies

Melt butter and marshmallows; add to Rice Krispies; butter hands and flatten in a 9x13 Tupperware.

Rainbow Finger Jell-O
Arlene Bontrager

6 (3 oz.) pkgs. assorted flavor Jell-O
6 Tbsp. Knox gelatin, divided
6 c. boiling water, divided
3 c. cold water, divided
1 (8 oz.) pkg. cream cheese,
   cut into 6 cubes

Mix 1 Tbsp. Knox gelatin with each flavor. (Mix with dry Jell-O only—before adding water!) In a bowl, dissolve 1 (3 oz.) Jell-O in 1 c. boiling water. Add ½ c. cold water; stir. Put half into a 10 inch Jell-O mold. Chill until almost set, about 40 minutes. Cool the other half of mixture, pour into blender. Add one cube of cream cheese, blend until smooth. Spoon over first layer, chill until set. Repeat 5 times, alternating plain Jell-O layer with creamed Jell-O layer and chilling between each step. Just before serving, unmold onto a serving platter. Note: This Jell-O takes time to prepare since each layer must be set before the next layer is added. Also remember the flavor you put in first will be on the top when unmolded.

Soft Pretzels
Emily Troyer

2 Tbsp. yeast
2 c. water
3½ Tbsp. brown sugar
1 Tbsp. white sugar
2 Tbsp. vegetable oil
4-6 c. flour

Mix dough. Let rise only 5 minutes. Roll into pretzel shape and dip in hot water that has 2 tsp. soda in it. Sprinkle with pretzel salt, let rise in pan. Bake at 400° until lightly brown.

Date Balls

Loma Kauffman

2½ c. butter
3 c. white sugar
7½ c. chopped dates
5 tsp. vanilla
8 eggs, well beaten
½ c. milk
1 tsp. salt
5 c. Rice Krispies
6 c. coconut

Heat sugar and butter until dissolved. Add dates; cook slowly until mushy, then add vanilla, eggs, milk, and salt. Cook 2 minutes. Remove from heat and let cool. Add Rice Krispies. Make balls and roll in coconut. Place on waxed paper and freeze. Makes a big batch.

Ice Cream Finger Jell-O

Emily Troyer

1½ c. Jell-O
2 Tbsp. gelatin
4 c. boiling water
2 c. ice cream

Mix Jell-O and gelatin; add boiling water. Stir until dissolved and add ice cream. Pour into a Jell-O mold and refrigerate.

Orange-Cream Fruit Mix

Emily Troyer

⅓ c. vanilla instant pudding
1½ c. milk
⅓ c. frozen orange juice
  concentrate
¾ c. sour cream

Mix pudding and milk; add rest of ingredients and beat. Mix with fresh fruit of your choice.

Swiss Roll Kabobs

Loma Kauffman

12 Swiss rolls
1 pt. fresh strawberries
6-8 kiwis
12 wooden skewers
fresh or canned chunk pineapples

Place carton of cakes in freezer for one hour. Freezing the cakes makes them easier to slice. Wash and slice all fruit and set aside. After the cakes have had time to freeze, slice and skewer, alternating with different fruits.

French Quarter Cheese
Mrs. Sheila Schrock

1 (8 oz.) pkg. cream cheese
½ tsp. minced garlic
1 tsp. minced onion
4 Tbsp. butter
¼ c. brown sugar
1 tsp. Worcestershire sauce
½ tsp. honey mustard
1 c. roasted, salted chopped pecans

Mix cream cheese, garlic, and onion. Spread on a plate in a thin layer. Cook together remaining ingredients. Spread on top of first layer. Chill several hours. Set out before serving time. Serve with crackers.

Creamy Chicken Spread
Brenda Beachy

1 (8 oz.) pkg. cream cheese, softened
½ c. sour cream
1 tsp. dried minced onion
½ tsp. onion salt
½ tsp. Worcestershire sauce
¼ tsp. red pepper
1½ lb. chicken breast, grilled and cubed

Mix together and serve with crackers.

Raspberry Mint Marshmallow Creme Dip
Amy Engbretson

4 oz. cream cheese, softened
1 c. marshmallow creme
⅔ c. vanilla or plain yogurt
½ c. fresh raspberries
2 tsp. fresh mint leaves, chopped
strawberries, kiwi, and pineapple

In medium bowl, beat cream cheese, marshmallow creme, yogurt, and raspberries with mixer on high speed until smooth. Stir in mint. Cover; refrigerate at least 2 hours but no longer than 12. Serve with strawberries, kiwi and pineapple. Serves 15 people.

BLT Dip
Emily Troyer

1 (8 oz.) pkg. cream cheese
¾ c. chopped lettuce
2 tomatoes, chopped
4 slices bacon, drained
   and crumbled

Spread cream cheese in a 9 inch pie pan. Top with lettuce and tomatoes; sprinkle with bacon. Serve with crackers or fresh veggies.

Taco Delight Dip
Mrs. Sheila Schrock

1 (8 oz.) pkg. cream cheese,
   softened
1 c. sour cream
1 tsp. Worcestershire sauce
1½ c. salsa
1 lb. ground beef, browned
½ pkg. taco seasoning
   (add to browned beef)
shredded lettuce
chopped onions
chopped tomatoes
chopped green peppers
1½ c. shredded cheddar cheese

Mix cream cheese and sour cream; add Worcestershire sauce. Spread on a large round tray. Layer hamburger on top, then spread with salsa. Layer remaining ingredients on top in order listed. Serve with tortilla chips or Doritos.

Warm Chicken Dip
Esta Miller

2 c. shredded chicken
1 can cream of chicken
1 c. cheddar cheese
1 can evaporated milk
½ c. celery
⅓ c. chopped onions
1 can green chilies
1 pkg. taco seasoning

Mix and heat everything together. Serve warm with tortilla chips.

Caramel Apple Dip

Mrs. Jeremy (Rose) Miller

1 c. butter
2 c. brown sugar
1 c. Karo
1 can Eagle Brand milk
½ tsp. cream of tartar

Mix all ingredients and boil on low heat for 2 minutes, stirring constantly. Can also be used as an ice cream topping, or boil for 5 minutes to make caramel candy. So good!

I have so much to do today that I have to take time to pray.

Meats and
Main Dishes

Notes

Chicken with Pineapple Sauce

Amy Engbretson

1 Tbsp. honey
1 Tbsp. cornstarch
1 (16 oz.) can pineapple, crushed or tidbits
¼ c. soy sauce
¼ tsp. garlic powder
¼ tsp. ground ginger

In saucepan, combine honey and cornstarch. Stir in remaining ingredients. Cook and stir over low heat till thickened. Use to cook chicken with, pour half over chicken and baste occasionally. Bake at 350° for 1 hour. Serve with rice.

Chicken Enchiladas

Emily Troyer

2 c. chopped, cooked chicken
1 green pepper, chopped
4 oz. cream cheese, cubed
½ c. salsa, divided
8 flour tortillas
¼ lb. Velveeta, chunked
1 Tbsp. milk

Mix first three ingredients and ¼ c. salsa in saucepan and heat until cream cheese is melted. Spoon ⅓ c. of mixture in tortillas and roll up. Place seam-side down in greased 9x13 pan. Heat Velveeta cheese and milk until cheese is melted and pour over tortillas. Bake 20 minutes and top with remaining salsa.

Chicken-N-Rice

Edith Engbretson

1 c. rice
1 can mushroom soup
2 c. chicken broth
1 pkg. onion seasoning mix
1 qt. canned chicken

Mix ingredients and bake for 45 minutes to an hour.

Poppy Seed Chicken
Arlene Bontrager

2 lb. chicken breast
1 (10½ oz.) cream of chicken soup
1 c. sour cream
½ c. butter, melted
1½ c. crushed Ritz crackers
poppy seeds to taste

Put 2 lb. of cooked chicken into a buttered 8x8 dish. Mix chicken soup and sour cream. Pour over chicken. Melt butter and add to crushed Ritz crackers. Put on top, sprinkle generously with poppy seeds, and bake at 350° for 40 minutes. Double ingredients for 9x13 pan.

Port-a-Pit Chicken
Arlene Bontrager

6 c. water
2½ Tbsp. Worcestershire sauce
2 tsp. garlic powder
¼ c. salt
1½ c. cider vinegar
½ c. brown sugar
6 Tbsp. margarine or butter
½ tsp. pepper

Mix together and boil 15 minutes. Add chicken and simmer 20 to 30 minutes. Grill chicken until done.

Poppy Seed Chicken
Ruth Bontrager

8 chicken breasts
2 (10 oz.) cans cream of chicken
16 oz. sour cream
3 c. Club cracker crumbs
1 c. margarine or butter
1 Tbsp. poppy seeds

Cut chicken breasts in strips and fry in olive oil. Season with Alpine Touch or salt. Put in a baking pan. Mix cream of chicken and sour cream. Put on top of chicken. Melt butter and mix with cracker crumbs and poppy seeds. Put on top of soup mixture. Bake at 350° for 45 minutes to 1 hour. Serves 6 to 8 people.

Stuffed Chicken Breast

Laura Ann Miller

6 boneless skinless chicken
  breasts, butterflied
½ c. butter, melted
4 oz. cream cheese
¾ c. milk
6 pcs. bacon
  Breading Mix:
4 c. flour
4 c. crushed crackers
2 Tbsp. salt
2 Tbsp. paprika
3 tsp. garlic salt
2 tsp. onion salt
2 Tbsp. sugar
can also use Runions

Brush chicken breasts with melted butter. Stuff with ½ inch chunk cream cheese; close and dip in melted butter and milk, then roll in breading mix. Wrap with bacon and secure with toothpick. Bake at 350° for 45 minutes. Serve immediately.

Rice on the Grill

Faith Ann Yoder

1½ c. uncooked rice
⅓ c. mushrooms
¼ c. chopped green peppers
¼ c. chopped onions
½ c. chicken broth
½ c. water
⅓ c. ketchup
1 Tbsp. butter

Combine the first seven ingredients in a foil pan, dot with butter. Cover with foil, seal edges tightly. Bake at 425°-450° for 14-15 minutes. Very good with grilled chicken!

To test a griddle, sprinkle a few drops of water onto it. If the water bounces, the pan is ready.

Chicken Fajitas
Faith Ann Yoder

Marinade:

¼ c. olive oil
3 Tbsp. fresh lime juice
2 Tbsp. red wine vinegar
2 Tbsp. finely chopped onion
½ tsp. sugar
½ tsp. dried oregano leaves
¼ tsp. salt
¼ tsp. black pepper

6 boneless skinless chicken
   breast halves
1 onion, cut into ½" slices
4 tomatoes, cut into ½" slices
1 pepper, cut into quarters
6 lg. flour tortillas
salsa or Ranch dressing

To Marinate: Combine the marinade ingredients; add chicken, turning to coat each side. Cover and refrigerate for 4 hours, turning occasionally. Grill the chicken breasts, onion, tomato and pepper slices over medium heat until the meat is no longer pink and the vegetables are tender, turning once. The chicken and onion will take 8-12 minutes and the tomato and pepper slices will take 6-8 minutes. Wrap tortillas in foil and place on cooking grate, heat for about 1 minute. Cut the pepper into strips and slice the chicken. Place chicken, onion, tomatoes and pepper in warm tortillas and roll up to eat. Serve with salsa or Ranch dressing. Serves 6 people.

Fried Chicken Strips
Mrs. Jerry Miller

2⅔ c. crushed saltines
   (approx. 80 crackers)
1 tsp. garlic salt
½ tsp. dried basil
½ tsp. paprika
⅛ tsp. pepper
1 egg
1 c. milk
1½ lb. boneless skinless chicken
   breasts, cut into ½" strips
oil for frying

In a shallow bowl, combine the first five ingredients. In another shallow bowl, beat egg and milk. Dip chicken into egg mixture, then cracker mixture. In an electric skillet or deep-fat fryer heat oil to 375°. Fry chicken, a few strips at a time, for 2-3 minutes on each side or until golden brown. Drain on paper towels.

Classic Lasagna Rolls

Mrs. Jerry Miller

12 lasagna noodles
1 lb. ground beef
1 c. chopped onion
2 cloves garlic, minced
1 (26 oz.) jar pasta sauce with herbs
1 (16 oz.) cont. ricotta cheese
1¼ c. shredded mozzarella cheese, divided
½ c. grated Parmesan cheese

Preheat oven to 350°. Coat a 9x13 baking dish with cooking spray. Prepare noodles according to package directions; drain noodles. Rinse with cool water; drain again. Lay noodles flat on waxed paper. Cook ground beef, onion, and garlic in a medium skillet over medium-high heat until meat is browned and crumbly, about 8 minutes. Drain fat from skillet. Add pasta sauce. Heat to boiling. Spread 2 c. of meat sauce into prepared baking dish. Mix ricotta and 1 c. mozzarella cheese in a large bowl. Spread cheese mixture over each noodle. Roll up noodles tightly; place seam side down on top of meat. Spoon remaining sauce on rolls; sprinkle with Parmesan cheese. Bake till heated through, about 30 minutes. Sprinkle with remaining mozzarella. Let set 5 minutes before serving. Serves 6 people.

Chicken Nuggets

Loma Kauffman

1 c. all-purpose flour
4 tsp. seasoned salt
1 tsp. paprika
1 tsp. poultry seasoning
1 tsp. ground mustard
½ tsp. pepper
8 boneless, skinless chicken breast halves
¼ c. vegetable oil

In a resealable plastic bag, combine the first six ingredients. Pound chicken to ½ inch thickness. Cut into 1½ inch pieces. Place chicken pieces, a few at a time, into bag and shake to coat. Heat oil in a skillet. Cook chicken, turning frequently until browned, about 6-8 minutes. Serves 8 people.

Chicken Breading
Arlene Bontrager

2 c. bread crumbs, fine
1½ tsp. salt
1½ tsp. paprika
1 tsp. celery salt
1 tsp. onion salt
¼ tsp. pepper
1 tsp. poultry seasoning
¼ c. vegetable oil

Mix well. Use for baking or deep-frying chicken. If you have leftover breading, keep in fridge, tightly covered.

Our Favorite Kabobs
Loma Kauffman

chicken breasts
elk steaks
red and green peppers
onions
fresh mushrooms
potatoes
carrots
zucchini squash
pineapple chunks
wooden skewers

Cut chicken breasts and steaks into bite size pieces and marinate in Italian dressing for 2 hours. Cube carrots and potatoes and cook for 5-8 minutes. Chunk up the rest of the vegetables and put on skewers alternately with the meat chunks. We like lots of meat. Grill until done. Soak the skewers in water at least 2-3 hours before using.

Breading for Chicken Breasts
Lorene Yoder

½ c. bread crumbs
⅛ c. Parmesan cheese
¼ c. shredded cheddar cheese
¼ tsp. basil
½ tsp. salt
¼ tsp. pepper
seasoned salt

Cut chicken breasts in 1 inch pieces; dip in melted butter, then in crumb mixture. Bake at 400° for 10 minutes or until done. Bake on cookie sheet or cake pan. Don't crowd together.

Chicken Gravy for Home (Lg. Recipe for Weddings)

4½ c. chicken broth
1½ Tbsp. chicken seasoning
⅛ tsp. garlic salt
5 Tbsp. clear jel
2 Tbsp. flour
1 egg
½ c. milk
  For 12 qt. Kettle:
2 gal. broth
5 Tbsp. chicken base
¼ tsp. garlic salt
salt and pepper to taste
  Gravy Paste:
2 eggs
1 c. pastry flour
1 c. cornstarch
enough milk to make 1 qt.

Bring chicken broth, chicken seasoning, and garlic salt to a boil. Make a paste with clear jel, flour, egg, and milk and whisk into hot broth. Bring to boil. Remove from oven. *For 12-quart Kettle:* Mix gravy paste in blender. Make 2 batches gravy paste for 12-quart kettle broth. Bring broth and seasonings to boil. Turn off heat and whisk in gravy paste. Mix well. Heat again just to boiling. Keep hot on simmer ring. Serve hot. Simple way to serve easy gravy.

Twice-Baked Potatoes

Emily Troyer

6 lg. baking potatoes
½ c. butter, softened
¾-1 c. milk
3 Tbsp. crumbled fried bacon
1 Tbsp. minced onion
1 Tbsp. snipped chives
½ tsp. salt
pepper
1½ c. shredded cheddar cheese, divided
paprika

Bake potatoes unwrapped on stove racks until soft. Cut lengthwise in half and scoop out soft pulp. Mash pulp and add butter. Blend in milk, bacon, onion, chives, salt, pepper, and 1 c. cheese. Refill shell and top with remaining cheese. Sprinkle with paprika. Bake at 375° for 30 minutes or until heated. Serves 6 people.

Jo-Jo Potatoes

Laura Ann Miller

6 med. potatoes,
   peeled and chunked, lengthwise
butter, melted
crushed cracker crumbs,
   mixed with seasoned salt

Dip potatoes in melted butter, then cracker crumbs. Bake at 350° for 45 minutes. Serve with ketchup. A family favorite!

Campfire Potatoes

Mrs. Marty (Esther) Miller

5 med. potatoes, peeled and
   thinly sliced
1 med. onion, sliced
6 Tbsp. butter
⅓ c. shredded cheddar cheese
2 Tbsp. parsley
1 Tbsp. Worcestershire sauce
salt and pepper to taste
⅓ c. chicken broth

Place the potatoes and onions on a large piece of heavy-duty foil (about 20x20 inch); dot with butter. Combine cheese, parsley, Worcestershire sauce, salt, and pepper; sprinkle over potatoes. Fold foil up around potatoes and add the broth. Seal foil tightly. Grill, covered, over medium heat for 35-40 minutes or until potatoes are tender. Open foil carefully to allow steam to escape. Serves 4 to 6 people.

Ranch Potatoes

Brenda Beachy

potatoes
salt
¼ c. butter
bacon bits
1 pkt. Ranch dressing mix
shredded cheese

Dice enough potatoes to fill a 12x18 pan. Boil with salt for 10 minutes in stockpot. Pour drained potatoes back into pan. Slice ¼ c. butter on top. Sprinkle with bacon bits. Pour 1 pkt. Ranch dressing mix (that has been mixed according to directions on pkt.) on top. Sprinkle with shredded cheese. Bake at 350° for 30 minutes.

Ranch Potatoes
Esta Miller

4½ lb. potatoes, boiled, cooled
  and shredded
2¼ c. milk
3 c. sour cream
3 pkg. Hidden Valley Ranch Mix
6 lb. hamburger
onion
3 pkg. taco seasoning
  Cheese Sauce:
1 c. butter
1 c. flour
8 c. milk
4 tsp. salt
4 c. Velveeta cheese

Heat together milk, sour cream, and Ranch mix. Mix with potatoes. Layer Ranch potatoes in Lifetime roaster. Fry hamburger and onion. Add taco seasoning and layer on top of potatoes. Cover with cheese sauce. *To Make Cheese Sauce:* Melt butter, then add flour. Slowly whisk in milk, salt, and Velveeta cheese. Last 10 minutes cover with taco chips (crumbled). Your roaster will be full to the brim. I prefer baking in a 200° oven for 4 hours to heat through. Serves 50 people.

Baked Spaghetti Squash
Mrs. Nancy Troyer

1 lb. hamburger, browned
1 onion, cut-up, optional
salt and pepper to taste
1 spaghetti squash

Cut spaghetti squash in half and deseed. Brown hamburger and onions. Put in spaghetti squash and bake at 350° for 2 hours. Top with cheese and serve with salsa and sour cream.

To prevent potatoes from boiling over, add a little butter.

Montana Cowgirl Casserole

Mary L. Troyer

1 lb. bulk sausage,
  browned and drained
½ lb. bacon, cooked and crumbled
12 oz. frozen hash brown potatoes
1 med. green pepper, chopped
2 Tbsp. chopped onion
2 c. shredded cheddar cheese
1 c. Bisquick or biscuit mix
3 c. milk
½ tsp. salt
4 eggs
vegetable oil or
  nonfat cooking spray

Oil 9x13 baking dish or spray with cooking spray. Combine sausage, bacon, hash browns, pepper, onions, and 1 c. cheese in a large bowl. Spread in a baking pan. Whisk together Bisquick, milk, salt, and eggs until well blended. Pour over potato mixture. Sprinkle with remaining cheese. Cover and refrigerate overnight (no longer than 24 hours). Next day: Bake uncovered for 30-35 minutes at 375° until light golden brown. Let set 10 minutes before serving. Serves 12 people.

Hobo's Delight

Brenda Beachy

2 lb. ground beef, browned
2 chopped onions
2 (6 oz.) cans tomato paste
1 qt. tomato juice
2 c. water
4 Tbsp. sugar
1 tsp. garlic powder
2 tsp. Ac`cent
2 tsp. chili powder
2 tsp. oregano
2 tsp. cumin
2 tsp. salt
½ c. raw rice
15 oz. can chili beans

Add all ingredients to browned beef and simmer till rice is tender (about 20 minutes). To serve make a stack. Layer in order: crushed corn chips, meat mixture, grated cheese, chopped tomatoes, shredded lettuce. Top with Hidden Valley Ranch dressing. Excellent dish to serve a crowd. Serves 10 people.

Reuben Crescent Bake
Amy Engbretson

2 (8 oz.) tubes crescent rolls
1 lb. sliced Swiss cheese
1¼ lb. sliced deli corned beef
1 can sauerkraut,
    rinsed and well drained
⅔ c. Thousand Island dressing
1 egg white, beaten
3 tsp. caraway seeds

Unroll one tube of crescent dough into a long rectangle. Seal seams and perforations. Press onto bottom of greased 9x13 pan. Bake at 375° for 8-10 minutes or until golden. Layer with half the cheese and all of the corned beef. Combine sauerkraut and salad dressing and spread over beef. Top with remaining cheese. On a lightly floured surface press or roll second tube of crescents. Place over cheese and brush with beaten egg white and sprinkle with caraway seeds. Bake for 12-16 minutes or till golden and heated through. Let set 5 minutes before cutting.

Pizza Casserole (A family favorite)
Dena Hostetler

1½ lb. hamburger
¼ c. onion
1½ c. cooked spaghetti
1 qt. pizza sauce
1 c. sour cream
3 Tbsp. salad dressing
2 c. grated cheese
1⅓ c. flour
2 tsp. baking powder
⅔ tsp. salt
½ c. milk
¼ c. vegetable oil

Fry hamburger with onions, put on bottom of 9x13 pan. Layer cooked spaghetti over meat and spread with pizza sauce. Mix sour cream, salad dressing, and cheese and spread over top. Last mix flour, baking powder, salt, milk, and vegetable oil, and spoon on top of sour cream spread. Bake at 350°, uncovered, until crust is done. Serves 12 people.

Fourth of July Casserole
Mrs. Floyd (Mollie) Yoder

4 pkts. beef flavored Ramen
  noodles
1 (8 oz.) can cream of mushroom
  soup
1 c. milk
½ lb. hamburger, fried and drained
2 slices bread
4 Tbsp. butter

Break noodles, then cook according to package directions. Add milk and cream of mushroom soup. Stir well. Put into a medium size casserole. Put hamburger on top of noodles. In a small skillet brown butter. Crumble bread slices into the butter. Stir. Sprinkle on top of casserole. Bake at 350° for 20 minutes. (This is a quick casserole if you get unexpected company.) Serves 6 people.

Taco Rice Casserole
Mrs. Sheila Schrock

1 lb. ground beef
½ pkg. taco seasoning
1 (15 oz.) can chili beans
1 pt. salsa
1 c. pizza sauce
4 c. cooked rice
1 c. butter
¾ c. flour
1 qt. milk
2-3 tsp. salt
Velveeta cheese

Fry beef, add taco seasoning, chili beans, salsa, and pizza sauce. Pour into 9x13 pan or other casserole dish. Spread cooked rice on top of meat. Melt butter and blend in flour, add milk, salt, and cheese to make a cheese sauce. Pour over top of rice. Bake at 350° for 30 minutes or until heated through. Top with crushed Doritos or chopped tomatoes and peppers to serve.

Sour Cream Noodle Casserole
Mrs. Nancy Troyer

4 oz. noodles, cooked
1 lb. hamburger, browned, seasoned
6 oz. mushrooms
cheese slices
8 oz. sour cream
2 cans cream of chicken soup

Put half of noodles, hamburger, mushrooms, and cheese in layers. Repeat layers. Mix the sour cream with soup and pour over all. Top with more cheese. Bake at 350° until hot. Serves 8 people.

Italian Spaghetti
Amy Engbretson

1 lb. hamburger
1 lg. onion, chopped (about 1 c.)
1 clove garlic, crushed
1 c. water
1 tsp. salt
1 tsp. sugar
1 tsp. dried oregano leaves
¾ tsp. dried basil leaves
½ tsp. dried marjoram leaves
¼ tsp. dried rosemary leaves,
   optional
1 bay leaf
1 (8 oz.) can tomato sauce
1 (6 oz.) can tomato paste
4 c. hot cooked spaghetti

Cook and stir hamburger, onion and garlic in skillet until hamburger is brown; drain. Stir in remaining ingredients except spaghetti. Heat to boiling; reduce heat. Cover and simmer, stirring occasionally, for 1 hour. Serve sauce over hot spaghetti. Sprinkle with Parmesan, if desired. Serves 6 people.

Layered Taco Delight
Laura Ann Miller

1 (8 oz.) pkg. cream cheese
1 c. sour cream
2 c. salsa
1 lb. hamburger, browned
1 pkg. taco seasoning
shredded lettuce
chopped onions
chopped tomatoes
chopped green peppers
1½ c. shredded cheddar cheese

Mix cream cheese and sour cream. Spread on a large round tray or in a Tupperware pan. Spread salsa on top. Mix hamburger and taco seasoning. Spread on top of salsa. Layer remaining ingredients in order given. Serve with tortilla chips.

Poor Man's Steak
Edith Engbretson

1 c. soda crackers
1 c. milk
1 lb. hamburger
1 onion, chopped
1 tsp. salt
½ tsp. pepper

Crush soda crackers and soak in the milk. Add rest of ingredients.

Meatballs

Edith Engbretson

2 eggs
1 c. oatmeal
½ c. milk
2 lb. hamburger
½ tsp. pepper
2 tsp. chili powder
½ tsp. garlic powder
3 tsp. salt
¼ c. onion
  Sauce:
3 c. ketchup
1½ c. brown sugar
½ tsp. garlic powder
1 Tbsp. minced onion

Beat eggs and add oatmeal and milk; let set a few minutes. Then add rest of ingredients. Put balls on a cookie sheet and pour sauce over them. Bake at 350° for 1 hour or until done.

Poor Man's Steak

Mrs. Steve (Linda) Kauffman

1½ lb. hamburger
½ c. cracker crumbs
½ c. cold water
2 tsp. salt
1 tsp. black pepper

Mix well and press into a pan 1 inch in thickness. Refrigerate overnight. Cut in squares. Roll in flour and fry in butter. Put in casserole or roaster and cover with one can of cream of mushroom soup, dilute the soup with some milk. Bake at 300° for 1½ hours. This is very tasty.

Marinated Grilled Steaks

Miriam Schlabach

1 c. olive oil
¼ c. red wine, optional
2 Tbsp. Worcestershire sauce
1 tsp. onion powder
1 tsp. garlic powder
pepper
parsley

Salt and pepper steaks and tenderize with meat mallet. Cover steaks with marinade and refrigerate ½ to 1 day. Cook on open fire grill until done.

Elk Roast
Mary L. Troyer

1 med. elk roast
1 pkg. onion soup mix
1 can cream of mushroom soup

Place roast on foil large enough to wrap meat tightly. Sprinkle roast with onion soup mix. Spoon cream of mushroom soup on top of roast, spreading evenly. Wrap tightly. Place in roasting pan and bake at 300° for 4 hours. This is a family favorite. Add mashed potatoes and gravy and you have a hearty meal!

Cheese-Stuffed Elk Loaf

1½ lb. ground elk
1 pt. pizza sauce
1 egg, slightly beaten
1 c. dry bread crumbs
2 tsp. Worcestershire sauce
½ tsp. salt
½ tsp. pepper
1 tsp. seasoned salt
chopped onion
2 c. shredded mozzarella cheese
1 Tbsp. finely chopped fresh parsley

Preheat oven to 350°. In a large bowl combine the first nine ingredients, putting in only ⅓ c. pizza sauce. In a 9x13 pan, shape the meat mixture into 8x12 inch rectangle. Sprinkle 1½ c. cheese and parsley down center, leaving ¾ inch border. Roll, starting at long end, jelly-roll style. Press ends together to seal. Bake uncovered for 45 minutes. Pour remaining sauce over meat loaf and sprinkle with remaining ½ c. cheese. Bake another 15 minutes. Let set 5 minutes before serving. Serves 6 people.

Barbecued Meatballs

Mrs. Kathryn Miller

3 lb. ground meat (venison or
   elk is good)
1 c. oatmeal
1 c. cracker crumbs
2 eggs
½ c. chopped onion
½ tsp. garlic powder
2 tsp. salt
½ tsp. pepper
2 tsp. chili powder
1 (12 oz.) can evaporated milk
  Sauce:
2 c. catsup
1 c. brown sugar
½ tsp. Liquid Smoke
½ tsp. garlic powder
¼ c. chopped onion

To make meatballs, combine all ingredients (mixture will be soft) and shape into walnut sized balls. Place meatballs in a single layer on wax paper lined cookie sheets. Freeze until solid. Store frozen meatballs in freezer bags until ready to cook. Yield: 80 meatballs. *To Make Sauce:* Combine all ingredients and stir until sugar is dissolved over low heat. Place frozen meatballs in a 13x9x2 baking pan. Pour on sauce and bake at 350° for 1 hour.

Steak Fajitas

Esther Yoder

1 lb. elk steak, cut into ¼" strips
   (or other meat of your choice)
1 med. onion, thinly sliced
1 sweet red pepper, thinly sliced
1 sweet yellow pepper, thinly sliced
2 Tbsp. olive oil
1 (1.25 oz.) pkg. Fajita seasoning
  mix
¼ c. water

Sauté onion and peppers in 2 Tbsp. olive oil until crisp-tender, remove and set aside. In same skillet cook steak for 4-6 minutes or until it reaches desired doneness. Return vegetables to pan, add seasoning mix and water. Simmer for 3-5 minutes. Serve on warm flour tortillas, top with salsa and sour cream.

Steak Marinade

Ruth Bontrager

1½ c. salad oil
¾ c. soy sauce
½ c. vinegar
⅓ c. lemon juice
2 tsp. salt
2 cloves garlic, crushed
4 Tbsp. Worcestershire sauce
2 Tbsp. dry mustard
2 tsp. parsley flakes
2 tsp. black pepper

Combine all ingredients. Stir to blend. Make this the day before using if possible. Makes 3 c. Two hours is the minimum to marinate a steak (beef, deer, or elk). Can also be used to marinate chicken breast. Great made on the grill.

Roast Beef Wraps

Amy Engbretson

½ c. sour cream
¼ c. Miracle Whip
salsa
10 (8") flour tortillas
10 lg. lettuce leaves
1 lb. thinly sliced roast beef
1 lb. thinly sliced cheddar cheese

Combine sour cream, Miracle Whip, and salsa. Spread over tortillas. Top with roast beef, cheese, and lettuce. Roll up tightly and secure with toothpicks. Cut in half. Serve with additional salsa, if desired. This is also good with any other combination of deli meat and cheese.

Chicken Fajita Pizza

Amy Engbretson

2 (14") pizza crusts
1 lb. boneless skinless chicken breasts, cut into strips
2 c. sliced onions
2 c. sliced green peppers
2 tsp. chili powder
1 tsp. garlic powder
1 c. salsa
2 c. shredded mozzarella cheese

In a skillet, sauté chicken in oil until juices run clear. Add onions, peppers, chili powder, garlic powder, and salt; cook until vegetables are tender. Spoon over crusts, top with salsa and cheese. Bake for 14-18 minutes or until crust is golden and cheese is melted. Yield: 2 pizzas, 8 slices each. Serves 8 people.

BLT Pizza

Amy Engbretson

Crust:

¾ c. water
2 Tbsp. vegetable oil
1 tsp. white sugar
½ tsp. salt
½ tsp. garlic powder
¼ c. Parmesan cheese
2½ c. flour
2¼ tsp. yeast

Topping:

½ c. salad dressing
2 tsp. basil, dried
½ tsp. garlic powder
⅓ tsp. onion powder

shredded lettuce
tomatoes, chopped
bacon
cheese

Crust Instructions: Mix yeast and sugar together, then add water. Let set till bubbly. Add the rest of the ingredients. Press or roll into round pizza pan. Let rise a little, then prebake at 400° for five minutes. Top with mixture of salad dressing, basil, and garlic and onion powder. Bake at 350° for 10-12 minutes or until golden. Remove from oven, then top with lettuce, tomatoes, bacon, and cheese. Serves 5 people.

Patience: The ability to idle your motor when you feel like stripping your gears.

Roasted Veggie Pizza

Amy Engbretson

2 sm. onions, sliced
16-20 med. fresh mushrooms, sliced
1 c. sliced green pepper
1 c. sliced sweet red pepper
4 tsp. olive oil
4 garlic cloves, minced
½ tsp. dried rosemary
½ tsp. dried oregano
½ tsp. dried thyme

Pesto Sauce:
1 Tbsp. coarsely chopped fresh basil
½ c. olive oil
½ c. Parmesan cheese
garlic cloves, minced
2 lg. tomatoes, thinly sliced
4 c. (16 oz.) shredded mozzarella cheese

1 (11x17) pizza crust (try Herb Pizza crust)

Place mushrooms, onions, and peppers in a roasting or baking pan lined with heavy-duty foil. Combine oil, garlic, rosemary, oregano, and thyme; drizzle over vegetables and toss to coat. Cover and bake at 400° for 20 minutes. Meanwhile, for sauce, combine basil, oil, Parmesan, and garlic in a food processor or blender; cover and process until smooth, scraping sides often. Set aside. Spread crust with sauce; top with tomato slices. Sprinkle with mozzarella cheese. Top with roasted vegetables.

Willpower: The ability to eat just one piece of chocolate!

Taco Pizza

Edith Engbretson

Crust:
½ c. warm water
1 pkg. yeast (or 1 Tbsp.)
1 tsp. sugar
1½ c. flour
1 Tbsp. vegetable oil
½ tsp. salt

Pizza Topping:
½ lb. beef
1 c. salsa
½ pkg. taco seasoning

Toppings:
2 c. cheese
2 c. shredded lettuce
1 c. onion
1 c. diced tomatoes

Make crust. Fry hamburger; add salsa and taco seasoning. Let crust rise, then put hamburger mixture on top. Sprinkle with ½ of cheese. Bake at 400° until edges are brown. Sprinkle with remaining cheese. Then top with the rest of toppings. Serve immediately.

Pizza Burgers

Mrs. Floyd (Mollie) Yoder

8 hamburger buns
1 lb. hamburger, fried, drained, and crumbled
1 lb. bologna, shredded
1 lb. Velveeta or American cheese, shredded
1 (26 oz.) jar spaghetti sauce

Put meats, cheese, and sauce into mixing bowl. Mix well. Lay bun halves on cookie sheet, face up. Spread sauce mixture on buns. Bake at 375° till cheese melts, approx. 10 minutes. Serves 16 people.

Pizza Subs

Amy Engbretson

8 lb. hamburger, browned with onions, drained, and chilled
1 lb. mozzarella cheese
¾ tsp. dried oregano
1½ qt. pizza sauce
80 slices American cheese
pepperoni
6-7 doz. sub buns

Mix first four ingredients together. For one sub, take a bun, put ½ slice cheese on it, then 2 scoops (#40 cookie) meat mixture, 3 slices pepperoni, and the other ½ slice cheese, then the top bun. Wrap in tinfoil and bake at 350° for 20-25 minutes. Let set for a few minutes, so buns get soft. Makes 6-7 dozen.

Beef and Mushroom Lasagna
Edith Engbretson

1 can cream of mushroom soup
¼ c. milk
1 lb. ground beef
2 c. pizza sauce
1 c. mushrooms
9 cooked lasagna noodles
1 c. shredded cheese

Stir milk and soup until smooth. Fry hamburger and stir in sauce and mushrooms. Layer beef mixture, then noodles, then soup mixture. Sprinkle with cheese. Bake for 45 minutes.

Pizza Lasagna
Lydiann Troyer

12 lasagna noodles, cooked and drained
2 (15 oz.) ricotta cheese
3 c. grated mozzarella, divided
5 oz. pepperoni, chopped
1 egg, beaten
1 Tbsp. fresh parsley, chopped
1½ tsp. dry spicy pizza seasoning
1½ qt. pizza sauce, divided
2 c. sausage, browned, divided
2 c. hamburger, browned, divided
¼ c. peppers, diced, divided
4 oz. mushrooms, chopped, divided
ham, optional

Preheat oven to 375°. In a bowl, combine ricotta cheese, 1½ c. mozzarella, chopped pepperoni, egg, parsley, and pizza seasoning. Spread ⅔ c. pizza sauce into 9x13 baking dish. Top with noodles, then drop 1⅓ c. ricotta cheese mixture by spoonfuls over noodles; gently spread. Layer 1 c. sausage, 1 c. hamburger (ham, optional), ⅛ c. peppers, and 2 oz. mushrooms. Spoon 1½ c. sauce over cheese mixture; lightly spread, making sure not to mix it with cheese. Repeat layers twice, ending with noodles. Cover with foil. Bake 45 minutes, or until bubbling. Sprinkle with remaining 1½ c. cheese, return to oven until cheese is melted.

Uncooked Lasagna

Mrs. Nancy Troyer

1 pkg. wide lasagna, uncooked
1 qt. spaghetti sauce
16 oz. cottage cheese
2 c. grated mozzarella cheese
2 lb. hamburger
1 med. onion
Parmesan cheese

Brown hamburger and onion and season with salt and pepper. In a large flat baking dish put a thin layer of meat and sauce. Place noodles on top of meat mixture and cheeses on top of that. Continue to layer until everything is used, beginning and ending with sauce; top with cheese. Bake at 350° for 1½ hour. Serves 10 people.

Best Barbecue Sauce

Mrs. Nancy Troyer

1 med. onion, cut-up
2 tsp. salt
¼ tsp. pepper
2 c. ketchup
1 Tbsp. chili powder
2 c. brown sugar
¼ c. Worcestershire sauce
¼ c. lemon juice
1 tsp. dry mustard
¼ tsp. garlic powder

Use for spareribs, chicken, or meatballs. Pour over your meat as it bakes.

Vegetables and Side Dishes

Notes

Before measuring honey or syrup, oil the cup with cooking oil and rinse in hot water.

Parmesan Potato Wedges
Esther Yoder

6 med. baking potatoes
¼ c. butter
¼ c. flour
¼ c. grated Parmesan cheese
salt and pepper to taste

Melt butter in large baking pan. Scrub potatoes and cut into sixths. Combine flour, cheese, and seasonings. Coat each potato wedge in this mixture, arrange in a single layer over butter and bake at 375° for 1 hour.

Campfire Potatoes
Lorene Yoder

5 med. potatoes, sliced
1 med. onion, sliced
⅓ c. chicken broth
2 Tbsp. fresh parsley
1 Tbsp. Worcestershire sauce
⅓ c. grated cheddar cheese
salt and pepper to taste

Place potatoes on heavy foil about 20x24 with onions and dot with butter. Combine other ingredients and sprinkle over potatoes. Seal edges well so broth stays in. Grill over medium coals for 30-40 minutes, until tender. Also may be done on campfire ashes. Serves 4 to 6 people.

Baked Basil Fries
Mrs. Steve (Linda) Kauffman

¼ c. grated Parmesan cheese
1 Tbsp. olive oil
1 Tbsp. dried basil
¼ tsp. garlic powder
4 med. red potatoes

In a bowl, combine Parmesan cheese, oil, basil, and garlic powder. Cut potatoes into ¼ inch sticks. Add to cheese mixture; toss to coat. Place in a buttered 15x10 baking pan. Bake at 425° for 15 minutes; turn potatoes. Bake 15-20 minutes longer or until crisp and tender. Serves 4 people.

Baked Potato Wedges
Edith Engbretson

6 potatoes, cut in 4 wedges
¾ c. butter, melted
1½ c. Runion breading
Parmesan cheese

Brush potatoes with butter and dip in breading. Sprinkle with Parmesan cheese. Bake at 400° for 30-40 minutes. Serve with honey mustard or sour cream.

Baked Potato Strips
Esta Miller

6 lg. potatoes, cut in strips
¼ c. vegetable oil
2 Tbsp. grated Parmesan
1½ tsp. salt
1 tsp. seasoned salt
½ tsp. garlic salt
1 tsp. paprika
½ tsp. pepper

Preheat oven to 500° and bake till soft, approximately 15 minutes.

Onion-Roasted Potatoes
Mrs. Jeremy (Rose) Miller

4 med. potatoes, cut into lg. chunks, about 2 lb.
⅓ c. olive oil
1 env. (1 oz.) onion soup and dip mix

Preheat oven to 425°. In 9x13 baking pan, combine all ingredients. Bake, stirring occasionally, 35 minutes or until potatoes are tender and golden brown. Great for any meal of the day. I often serve these with blueberry French toast for brunch. Serves 4 people.

Spicy Potato Wedges
Amy Engbretson

¼ c. vegetable or olive oil
1 Tbsp. chili powder
2 tsp. onion powder
2 tsp. garlic salt
1 tsp. sugar
1 tsp. paprika
¾ tsp. salt
¼-½ tsp. red pepper, optional
3½ lb. lg. potatoes, cut in wedges

In a large bowl, combine everything but potatoes. Add potatoes and stir to coat. Arrange in a single layer on greased baking sheets. Bake 15 minutes at 400° then flip and bake till done, 15-20 more minutes. Serves 8 people.

Herbed New Potatoes
Mary L. Troyer

12 sm. new potatoes
4 tsp. butter
4 tsp. minced fresh parsley or
 1½ tsp. dried
4 tsp. minced fresh chives or
 1½ tsp. dried
fresh parsley sprigs for garnish

Peel 1½ inch strip around the center of each potato. In a medium saucepan, boil potatoes until almost soft. Do not overcook. Drain and keep warm. Meanwhile, melt butter and stir in fresh herbs. Pour butter mixture over potatoes and toss to coat. Spoon potatoes into serving bowl, garnish with parsley and serve immediately. For variety sprinkle with chopped cooked bacon and/or Parmesan cheese and finely minced green onion. Serves 4 people. Montana is known for its wonderful potatoes. We prefer the red.

Baked Potato Topping
Sarah Ann Miller

1 lb. hamburger
½ c. chopped onion
1 (10½ oz.) can tomato soup
1 (10½ oz.) can mushroom soup
½ lb. Velveeta cheese
1 tsp. chili powder
1 tsp. onion powder
1 tsp. garlic powder
baked potatoes

Brown hamburger with onions. Drain grease. Stir in soups, cheese, and seasonings. Simmer 30 minutes.

Carrots Au Gratin
Mrs. Floyd (Mollie) Yoder

3 c. cooked carrots, diced
 and drained
1 (8 oz.) can cream of celery soup
1 c. shredded Velveeta cheese
¼ c. bread crumbs
1 Tbsp. butter, melted

In a 1 quart casserole, combine carrots, soup, and cheese. Top with bread crumbs that have been toasted in melted butter. Bake at 350° for 20-25 minutes. Serves 6 people.

Corn Casserole
Miriam Schlabach

½ c. butter
1 sm. onion
½ green pepper
1 can whole corn, undrained
1 can creamed corn
1 Jiffy corn muffin mix
3 eggs
½ pt. sour cream
1 c. sharp cheese

Sauté the onion and pepper in butter. Combine corn, muffin mix, eggs, sour cream, and cheese. Add the vegetables. Pour into greased 9x9 pan. Bake at 350° for 1 hour.

Zucchini Quiche
Lorene Yoder

3 c. shredded zucchini
1 c. Bisquick mix
½ c. chopped onions
½ c. Parmesan cheese
2 Tbsp. parsley
½ tsp. salt
½ tsp. pepper
½ tsp. oregano
4 eggs, beaten
½ c. cooking oil

Beat eggs; add rest of the ingredients. Put into greased 9x9 pan and bake at 350° for 45-50 minutes. Serves 4 to 6 people.

Coney Sauce
Edith Engbretson

2 Tbsp. flour
2 Tbsp. butter
1 lb. fried hamburger
1 c. ketchup
½ c. barbecue sauce
1 Tbsp. mustard
¼ c. brown sugar
1 onion, chopped

Brown flour in butter; add rest of ingredients. Simmer for 15 minutes.

Soups, Salads and Dressings

Notes

Navy Bean Soup

Mrs. Steve (Linda) Kauffman

1 lb. dried navy beans
2 Tbsp. salt
water
1 can beef or chicken broth
1 chicken bouillon cube
4 potatoes, peeled and diced
2 onions, diced
¼ c. butter
4 carrots, sliced
2 c. ham, chopped
salt to taste
pepper to taste

Rinse beans and place in a large stockpot. Cover with water. Add salt and soak overnight. Drain. Bring 5 c. water, broth, and bouillon cube to a boil. Reduce heat and simmer for 2 hours. Add potatoes, carrots, and ham. In a separate saucepan sauté onions in butter. Add to soup. Season with salt and pepper. Add more water if desired. Simmer until vegetables are tender. Serve with fresh bread and a green salad. Serves 8 people.

Cheesy Chicken Chowder

Mrs. Sheila Schrock

3 c. chicken broth
2 c. peeled and diced potatoes
1 c. diced carrots
1 c. diced celery
1 c. diced onion
1 tsp. salt
¼ tsp. pepper
¼ c. butter or margarine
⅓ c. flour
2 c. milk
2 c. Velveeta or cheddar cheese
2 c. cooked and diced chicken

In a 4 quart saucepan bring chicken broth to a boil. Reduce heat; add potatoes, carrots, celery, onion, salt, and pepper. Cover and simmer 20 minutes. Meanwhile, melt butter in a medium saucepan, add flour and mix well. Gradually stir in milk; heat over low heat till slightly thickened. Add cheese. Add this to broth along with chicken. Stir until heated through. Serves 8 people.

"The Best" Chili Soup
Esta Miller

2 qt. tomato soup
1 can kidney beans
1 can pork and beans
2 Tbsp. mustard
1½ c. brown sugar
2 lb. hamburger
1 onion
1 tsp. salt
¼ c. ketchup
6 tsp. chili powder

I use my home canned Campbell's tomato soup. This chili is hard to beat! Fills 6 quart kettle to the brim. Take this recipe 5x to fill a 20 quart canner if you want to can a large batch.

Amy's Chili Soup
Amy Engbretson

1 lb. hamburger
1 tsp. salt
½ tsp. pepper
2 tsp. Italian seasoning
1 qt. pizza sauce
1 pt. tomato juice (may add more)
1 can kidney beans, optional
½ c. brown sugar
1½ tsp. chili powder

Brown hamburger; add salt, pepper, and seasoning. Add rest of ingredients and stir. May add more seasonings to taste. Delicious! Serves 6 people.

Ham and Potato Soup
Emily Troyer

2 c. thinly sliced raw potatoes
2 c. boiling water
¼ tsp. Worcestershire sauce
1 c. chopped ham
¼ c. finely chopped onion
1½ c. milk
1 Tbsp. butter
1 c. Velveeta cheese, cut up
1 tsp. salt
pepper

Add potatoes, ham, and onions to boiling water. Cover and cook until potatoes are tender. Mash potatoes slightly with a fork to thicken soup. Add milk, butter, and seasonings. Heat; add cheese before serving.

Country Potato Soup
Fannie Yoder

3 c. diced potatoes
½ c. carrots
½ c. onion, optional
1½ c. water
1 Tbsp. chicken base
1 Tbsp. parsley flakes
1 c. sour cream
2 Tbsp. flour
2 c. milk
salt and pepper to taste
½ lb. ham, cubed
½ lb. Velveeta cheese

Cook potatoes, carrots, onions, ham, water, chicken base, salt, and pepper in large saucepan until tender. Add 1 c. milk. Blend sour cream and flour, then add remaining milk. Gradually add to soup base. Cook over low heat, stirring constantly, until thickened. Add parsley flakes and cheese. May also use sausage or hamburger.

Bacon Potato Soup
Mrs. Amy Miller

8 strips bacon
2 c. cubed potatoes
1 c. onions
1 c. water
½ tsp. salt
1 (10 oz.) can cream of mushroom
  soup
1 c. sour cream
1¾ c. milk
½ lb. Velveeta cheese
2 Tbsp. parsley
pepper to taste

Fry bacon. In a large saucepan combine bacon grease, water, potatoes, onions, and salt. Cook till potatoes are tender. Add soup, sour cream, milk, parsley, cut-up bacon, and cheese. Heat until cheese is melted, but don't let it cook again.

Summer Pasta Salad

Esther Yoder

½ lb. Rotini pasta
1 green pepper, chopped
1 c. cherry tomatoes
½ c. cooked green peas
½ c. diced cheddar cheese
¼ c. bacon bits
1 (2.25 oz.) can sliced black olives
  Dressing:
¼ c. Italian dressing
¼ c. Ranch dressing
2 Tbsp. sugar
½ tsp. salt

Cook pasta until tender, cool. Drain. Add remaining ingredients. *For Dressing:* Mix all ingredients together. Toss salad with dressing.

Three-Bean Salad

Dena Hostetler

½ c. vegetable oil
½ c. apple cider vinegar
¾ c. sugar
1½ tsp. salt
½ tsp. pepper
1 can green beans, drained
1 can yellow beans, drained
1 c. mixed dried beans,
  soaked until soft
1 can red kidney beans, drained
1 red onion, chopped
cauliflower buds

Mix all together, refrigerate and enjoy. Very delicious! Serves 15 people.

Herbed Tomatoes
Amy Engbretson

1 c. olive oil
⅓ c. vinegar
¼ c. fresh parsley or 3 Tbsp. dried
1 Tbsp. basil or 3 Tbsp. fresh
1 Tbsp. sugar
1 tsp. salt
½ tsp. fresh ground pepper
½ tsp. dry mustard
½ tsp. garlic powder
1 sm. onion
tomatoes

Cut up tomatoes and onion; marinate for at least 3 hours before serving. Very good with cottage cheese and French dressing or use for tomato sandwiches (well drained). More tomatoes may be added to marinade, once or twice, until it gets too weak.

Taco Salad
Amy Engbretson

1 head lettuce
1 lg. onion, optional
1 lb. hamburger
4 med. tomatoes
8 oz. cheddar cheese
1 bag Doritos or taco chips
1 can kidney beans
2 tsp. taco seasoning
  Dressing:
16 oz. Thousand Island dressing
½ c. sugar
⅓ c. ketchup
2 tsp. taco seasoning mix
¾ c. water

Brown meat and season with taco seasoning. Mix all ingredients except chips in bowl. *For Dressing:* Mix all ingredients with whisk. When ready to serve, toss salad with dressing and add chips. Serves 6 people.

BLT Salad

Brenda Beachy

1 head lettuce
8 slices bacon
2 hard-boiled eggs
1 c. shredded cheese
2 c. croutons
1 pt. cherry tomatoes
  Dressing:
½ c. sugar
1 tsp. mustard
1 Tbsp. vinegar
1 c. mayonnaise
1 Tbsp. milk

Toast bread cubes in butter. Sprinkle with seasoning salt. Put on cookie sheet and crisp in oven. Mix dressing ingredients and pour over salad.

Bacon Chicken Salad

Amy Engbretson

2 heads lettuce
some spinach
4 hard-boiled eggs
20 pcs. bacon, fried and crumbled
2-3 lb. chicken breast,
   cubed and fried
cheddar cheese
  Dressing:
1¼ c. Miracle Whip
⅔ c. barbecue sauce
2 Tbsp. lemon juice
6 Tbsp. sugar
1 tsp. salt
½ tsp. pepper
½ tsp. Liquid Smoke, optional

Mix all ingredients in Fix 'n Mix bowl. Toss and serve.

Texas Salad
Loma Kauffman

2 c. sliced olives
2 c. slivered almonds, toasted
2 c. sunflower seeds, toasted
½ c. chopped peppers
1½ c. chopped celery
1¼ c. shredded cheese
8 c. cooked macaroni shells
1 c. chopped onions
Dressing:
1 c. vinegar
1 c. vegetable oil
1¾ c. white sugar
1¾ c. brown sugar
2 Tbsp. chicken base
¾ Tbsp. soy sauce
1 c. oyster sauce
¾ Tbsp. black pepper
2 Tbsp. chili powder
2 tsp. celery salt

Blend all dressing ingredients in blender except oil. Add oil in a slow stream. Combine all vegetables and macaroni in a big bowl. Toss with dressing and nacho chips or corn chips.

Overnight Potato Salad
Arlene Bontrager

12 c. cooked potatoes
12 eggs, cooked
1½ c. chopped onion
1½ c. chopped celery
3 c. mayonnaise
3 Tbsp. vinegar
3 Tbsp. mustard
4 tsp. salt
2 c. sugar
½ c. milk

Chop and mix the first four ingredients together. Then mix the rest of the ingredients together; mix well. Then mix with potatoes, eggs, onion, and celery. Let set overnight.

Dressing for Coleslaw

Arlene Bontrager

1 c. salad dressing
½ c. sugar
1 tsp. garlic powder
1 tsp. celery seed
1 tsp. salt
2 tsp. vinegar

Shred one medium head of cabbage.

Layered Salad Plate

Mrs. Floyd (Mollie) Yoder

1 head lettuce, shredded
1 med. onion, chopped
1 green pepper, chopped
2 c. diced tomatoes
8 hard-boiled eggs
1 c. Miracle Whip salad dressing
1 Tbsp. vinegar
⅔ c. sugar
4 slices fried bacon, crumbled
½ c. shredded cheese

On a large plate, layer the first four items given. Mash eggs in a bowl with the potato masher. Add salad dressing, vinegar, and sugar to eggs. Mix well. Top with shredded cheese and bacon. Serves 15 to 20 people.

Tomatoes and Cukes

Mrs. Nancy Troyer

2 Tbsp. vegetable oil
1 Tbsp. vinegar
1 Tbsp. minced parsley
¼ tsp. salt
¼ tsp. pepper
3 med. tomatoes, sliced
½ lg. cucumber, sliced
1 lg. onion, sliced, optional
leaf lettuce

In a small bowl, whisk oil, vinegar, parsley, salt, and pepper. On a serving plate, arrange tomato and cucumber slices over lettuce. Drizzle with the vinaigrette. Serves 4 people.

Sour Cream Coleslaw

Edith Engbretson

3 heads cabbage, shredded
2 peppers, chopped
2 carrots, shredded

1½ c. sour cream
1½ c. mayonnaise
1½ c. sugar
4 Tbsp. vinegar
½ Tbsp. celery seed
3 tsp. salt

Mix cabbage, peppers, and carrots. Mix remaining ingredients for dressing. This will keep for 2 weeks.

Coleslaw

Ruth Bontrager

4-6 c. shredded cabbage
1 sm. can pineapple, crushed or chunk
1 carrot, shredded
½ c. chopped walnuts, optional
1 c. mayonnaise
1-2 Tbsp. seasoned rice vinegar
salt, pepper, and sugar to taste
milk to make dressing slightly liquid, not too thin

Mix together and serve.

If you can't find time to do a job right, when will you find time to do it over?

Holiday Ribbon Salad
Esther Yoder

6 oz. lime gelatin
6 oz. cherry gelatin
3 oz. lemon gelatin
1 c. miniature marshmallows
8 oz. cream cheese
1 lb. 4 oz. can crushed pineapple
8 oz. whipped topping

First Layer: Mix lime gelatin according to package directions; pour into 10x14 glass pan and chill until set. *Second Layer:* Dissolve lemon gelatin in ½ c. hot water; add marshmallows and stir over low heat until melted. Remove from heat; add cream cheese, and pineapple. Chill until cool and starting to thicken, then fold in whipped topping. Pour onto lime layer and chill until set. *Third Layer:* Mix cherry gelatin according to package directions, chill until just starting to set (syrupy texture is preferred) pour on top of second layer. Pretty and refreshing.

The Greatest Fruit Salad
Laura Ann Miller

1 lg. box vanilla instant pudding
1½ c. milk, heated and cooled
6 oz. frozen orange juice
    concentrate or pineapple juice
¼ c. sour cream

Combine pudding mix, milk, and orange juice in bowl. Beat for 2 minutes. Blend in sour cream; mix well. Pour over mixed fruit—peaches, strawberries, apples, grapes, bananas, mandarin oranges, and pineapple.

Minty Fruit Salad
Lorna Kauffman

2 c. cubed honeydew
2 c. halved strawberries
1 c. sliced bananas
1 c. grapefruit segments
1 c. sliced halved peeled kiwifruit
1 c. mandarin oranges
½ c. sugar
⅓ c. orange juice
⅓ c. lemon juice
⅛ tsp. peppermint extract

In a large bowl, combine the fruit. In a small bowl combine the remaining ingredients. Pour over fruit and gently stir to coat. Cover and refrigerate for at least 3 hours. Serves 8 people.

Italian Dressing
Amy Engbretson

¼ c. lemon juice
¼ c. vinegar
¾ c. olive oil
1 tsp. honey, optional
½ tsp. garlic powder
½ tsp. onion powder
1 tsp. salt
½ tsp. ground mustard
½ tsp. ground oregano
½ tsp. dried basil
¼ tsp. paprika
½ tsp. kelp, optional

Mix in blender or bowl. Delicious!

Poppy Seed Dressing
Amy Engbretson

1 c. sugar
½ c. vinegar
1 Tbsp. onion
½ tsp. salt
1½ c. vegetable oil
2 Tbsp. poppy seeds
¾ c. Miracle Whip
1 c. sour cream

Mix first five ingredients, then add remaining ingredients. Beat well. Equals about a quart.

Tips and Hints

When making angel food cakes use eggs at room temperature. You will obtain a top-quality cake by using cake flour. However, if you don't have any and are using all-purpose flour, remove 2 Tbsp. per cup used, and add 2 Tbsp. cornstarch instead.

Drop a cut-up potato into a pot of soup or stew that is too salty. The potato will absorb the salt.

If you have problems with rough and scabby potatoes, try rolling your seed potatoes that have been cut in garden sulfur before planting. They will grow nice and smooth.

Sewing tip for hemming a dress, apron or outside edge of cape. Sew in long stitch (5) however deep you will have your fold. Press line right where you sewed, now you are ready to hem. When done, pull out the long stitch. Fast and accurate.

To keep dishcloths from getting smelly, rinse well in hot water and then in cold water after each use.

To keep celery fresh wrap in wet paper towel. Put tinfoil around and store in refrigerator.

Rice will be fluffier and whiter if you add 1 tsp. of lemon juice to each quart water.

Add some vinegar to your water when you cold pack to eliminate the need of washing the jars.

When baking potatoes, bake extra. Cool and put through shoe string salad master. Freeze in ziplock bags. These are delicious for home fries or any potato casserole. So convenient! A must for the freezer.

No need to plant your potatoes deep. As soon as they start growing, hill them, covering the whole plant. Do this each time they grow out until no longer possible. Your potatoes will roll out of the mound at the end of the season. Try it!

Desserts

Notes

Pumpkin Torte

Layer 1:
24 graham crackers, crushed
½ c. butter
½ c. sugar
Layer 2:
2 eggs, beaten
¾ c. sugar
8 oz. cream cheese or sour cream
Layer 3:
2 c. pumpkin
3 eggs, separated
¾ c. sugar, divided
1 Tbsp. unflavored gelatin
½ c. milk
½ tsp. salt
1 Tbsp. cinnamon
8 oz. whipped topping, divided

Layer 1: Mix and press into 9x13 pan. *Layer 2:* Mix and pour over crust. Bake at 350° for 20 minutes. *Layer 3:* Cook pumpkin, egg yolks, ½ c. sugar, milk, salt, and cinnamon until it thickens. Remove from heat and add gelatin dissolved in cold water, cool. Beat egg whites and ¼ c. sugar. Beat into pumpkin mixture. Add 1 c. whipped topping. Pour over cooled crust. Top with rest of whipped topping.

If you want to feel rich, count all of the things you have that money can't buy.

Huckleberry Roly-Poly
Mary L. Troyer

½ c. shortening
½ c. brown sugar
1 egg
½ c. maple syrup
2¼ c. flour
½ tsp. salt
½ tsp. soda
½ c. boiling water
1 tsp. cinnamon
½ tsp. nutmeg
1½ c. fresh huckleberries
 Sauce:
1 c. sugar
1 Tbsp. flour
½ c. cold water
¼ tsp. salt
1 egg, beaten
1 Tbsp. butter
¼ c. sweet cream
1 tsp. vanilla

Cream together shortening and sugar. Add egg and syrup and beat. Sift flour; add salt and spices and mix dry ingredients together. Dissolve soda in boiling water. Add dry ingredients alternately with hot water. Fold in floured berries. Pour into greased 9x9 square pan. Bake at 350° for 35 minutes. Serve warm with sauce. *To Make Sauce:* Combine flour and sugar. Slowly add cold water and stir to a smooth paste. Bring to a boil and cook for 3 minutes, stirring constantly. Add beaten egg; boil 1 minute longer. Remove from heat and add butter, sweet cream, and vanilla. Stir until well blended. Serves 6 to 8 people.

Pumpkin Roll
Rachel Troyer

3 eggs, beaten
1 c. sugar
⅔ c. pumpkin
1 tsp. salt
1 tsp. soda
1 tsp. cinnamon
¾ c. flour
 Filling:
1 (8 oz.) pkg. cream cheese,
 softened
2 tsp. butter
1 tsp. vanilla
1 c. powdered sugar

Mix together and spread on a greased and floured 12x17 cookie sheet. Bake at 375° for 15 minutes. As soon as it's done, turn out onto a powdered sugared surface; roll up like a jelly roll until cooled. *For Filling:* Blend cream cheese and butter until smooth. Add vanilla and powdered sugar. Unfold pumpkin roll and spread with filling. Roll up again; slice in ¾ inch slices and serve.

Plum Bumble

Sarah Ann Miller

1 c. plus 5 tsp. sugar, divided
¼ c. cornstarch
3 c. sliced fresh plums
¾ c. pineapple tidbits
2 Tbsp. butter, divided
½ tsp. ground cinnamon
1 (7½ oz.) tube refrigerated
   buttermilk biscuits, separated
   and quartered

In a bowl, combine 1 c. sugar, cornstarch, plums, and pineapple. Transfer to a greased shallow 2 quart baking dish; dot with 1 Tbsp. butter. Bake uncovered at 400° for 15 minutes. Meanwhile, melt remaining butter. In a small bowl, combine cinnamon and remaining sugar. Place biscuit pieces over hot plum mixture; brush with butter and sprinkle with cinnamon-sugar. Bake 25-30 minutes longer or until biscuits are golden brown. Serves 6 people.

Flip-Over Apple Cake

Lorene Yoder

½ c. unsalted butter
4 med. apples
1 Tbsp. ground cinnamon
1 c. plus 1 Tbsp. sugar
1 c. all-purpose flour
1 egg, beaten
1½ c. chopped walnuts, optional
mint sprigs, optional

Preheat oven to 350°. Generously grease a 9 inch round cake pan with butter. Melt ½ c. butter in saucepan. Set aside to cool. Peel, core, and cut apples into ¼ inch slices. Place apples in bowl, toss to coat with cinnamon and 1 Tbsp. sugar. Place apple slices in bottom of pan. Sift remaining 1 c. sugar and the flour in large bowl. Whisk in egg and melted butter just until combined; add nuts (don't overmix). Spread evenly over the apples. Bake about 40-45 minutes. Cool. Loosen around pan and invert onto serving plate. Can be served with whipped cream or ice cream. Serves 10 people.

Lemon Lush

Saloma Kurtz (age 10)

1 c. flour
½ c. butter
½ c. pecans
1 (8 oz.) pkg. cream cheese
1 c. powdered sugar
1 c. Cool Whip
2 c. sugar
⅓ c. cornstarch
¼ tsp. salt
¼ c. water
¼ c. lemon juice
¼ c. vinegar
1¾ c. water
3 eggs
1 Tbsp. butter
1 tsp. lemon extract

Mix together flour, butter, and pecans and press into greased pan. Bake at 375° for 15 minutes. Beat together cream cheese, powdered sugar, and Cool Whip and pour over crust. Chill. Cook together next eight ingredients and add butter and lemon extract. Lemon lovers' favorite dessert.

Brownie Ice Cream Dessert

Mrs. Sheila Schrock

1 lb. butter
1 lb. chocolate chips
6 lg. eggs
2¼ c. white sugar
2 Tbsp. vanilla
1 c. Gold Medal flour
1 Tbsp. baking powder
1 tsp. salt

Melt butter and chocolate chips. Do not boil, cool. In a large bowl beat the eggs, then add sugar and vanilla; add chocolate mixture. Mix well and add flour, baking powder, and salt. Spread in a greased 10x15 pan. Bake at 350° for 20 minutes. Shake or pat bottom of pan, then bake another 15 minutes or until done. Do not overbake, but make sure they're done. Cool. Then cut into 1 inch squares. Layer in large bowl with ice cream "scoops", and drizzle with caramel or hot fudge sauce.

Cream Cheese Squares

Edith Engbretson

1 (8 oz.) tube crescent rolls
16 oz. cream cheese, softened
⅔ c. white sugar
1 tsp. vanilla

1 (8 oz.) tube crescent rolls
¼ c. butter, melted
⅔ c. white sugar
1 tsp. cinnamon

Put first tube of crescent rolls in the bottom of a 9x13 pan. Stretch to fit. Blend next three ingredients together and spread over rolls. Place next tube of rolls on top. Brush with butter. Sprinkle with white sugar and cinnamon (mixed).

Frozen Peanut Butter Dessert

Emily Troyer

1 (8 oz.) pkg. cream cheese
⅔ c. peanut butter
2 c. powdered sugar
1 c. milk
6 c. whipped topping
  Crumbs:
2 pkgs. graham crackers
4 Tbsp. brown sugar
⅓ c. butter

Mix crumbs; put ½ of mixture in a 9x13 pan. Cream together first three ingredients, then add milk. Fold in whipped topping and spread on crumbs. Sprinkle rest of crumbs on top and freeze.

To prevent stringy tapioca, don't stir while cooling.

Banana Split Supreme
Emily Troyer

¾ c. butter, divided
2 c. powdered sugar
1 c. evaporated milk
¾ c. chocolate chips
24 Oreo cookies, crushed
3-4 bananas, cut in slices
2 qt. vanilla ice cream, softened
    and divided
1 can crushed pineapple
1 jar maraschino cherries,
    drained and halved
¾ c. pecans, chopped
whipped topping

Combine ½ c. butter, sugar, milk, and chocolate chips. Bring to a boil over medium heat; boil and stir for 8 minutes. Remove from heat and cool completely. Meanwhile, melt the remaining butter; toss with cookie crumbs. Press in a greased 13x9x2 pan. Freeze for 15 minutes. Arrange banana slices over crust; spread with one quart ice cream. Top with one cup of chocolate sauce. Freeze for 1 hour. Refrigerate remaining sauce. Spread remaining ice cream over dessert; top with pineapples, cherries, and pecans and freeze. Ten minutes before serving, heat remaining sauce and drizzle over the top and add dabs of whipped topping. Serves 12 to 15 people.

Frozen Raspberry Dessert
Amy Engbretson

2 c. Oreos, crushed
⅓ c. butter, melted
1 c. hot fudge topping
1 qt. vanilla ice cream
1 pt. raspberry sherbet
frozen raspberries
1 (8 oz.) cont. Cool Whip

Mix together melted butter and Oreos and put in 9x13 pan. Put hot fudge on top of Oreo crust, then layer remaining ingredients in order given. Garnish with a few raspberries. Freeze.

Reese's Dessert
Faith Ann Yoder

1 (16 oz.) pkg. Oreo cookies
¼ c. butter, melted
1 (8 oz.) pkg. cream cheese
powdered sugar
½ c. peanut butter
8 oz. Cool Whip
3 c. milk
1 sm. pkg. instant vanilla pudding
1 sm. pkg. instant chocolate
   pudding
additional Cool Whip
Reese's peanut butter cups

Crush the Oreo cookies; add melted butter. Press crumbs into bottom of 9x13 pan for the crust. Cream together cream cheese, powdered sugar, and peanut butter; add 8 oz. Cool Whip. Put mixture on top of cookie layer. Sprinkle with Reese's cups. Chill. Mix milk with both packages of instant pudding. Pour on top of cream cheese layer. When set, top with additional Cool Whip and sprinkle with Reese's cups.

Cherry Cheesecake
Ruth Bontrager

2 (8 oz.) pkg. cream cheese,
   softened
3½ c. milk, divided
2 (3 oz.) pkg. vanilla instant
   pudding
1 (9x13) pan graham cracker crust
2 (2 oz.) cherry pie filling

Beat cream cheese until soft. Blend in 1 c. milk until very smooth. Add 2½ c. milk and pudding mix. Blend about 1 minute. Pour on crust. Cover with cherry pie filling. May use any flavor pudding and pie filling; lemon pudding with blueberry filling or ½ orange dream and ½ vanilla with peach filling are delicious.

Easy Chocolate Lovers' Cheesecake
Mrs. Amy Miller

3 (8 oz.) pkg. cream cheese, softened
¾ c. sugar
3 eggs
1 tsp. vanilla
2 c. chocolate chips, divided
1 extra-serving size graham cracker crust

Heat oven to 450°. Beat cream cheese and sugar in large bowl with mixer until well blended. Add eggs and vanilla; beat well. Stir in 1½ c. small chocolate chips; pour into crust. Bake 10 minutes. Without opening oven door reduce temperature to 250°; continue baking 30 minutes or just until set. Remove from oven to wire rack. Sprinkle remaining ½ c. chocolate chips over hot cheesecake. Spread even when they are melted. Cool. Cover and refrigerate until completely chilled. Serves 10 people.

Cheesecake
Ella Yutzy

3 oz. pkg. lemon orange Jell-O
1 c. boiling water
1 (8 oz.) pkg. cream cheese
1 c. sugar
1 Tbsp. lemon juice
4 c. whipped topping
3 c. graham crackers
½ c. butter, melted

Dissolve Jell-O in hot water; chill until slightly thickened. Cream together cream cheese, sugar, and lemon juice, then blend into Jell-O. Fold in the whipped topping. Mix graham cracker crumbs and butter. Press ⅔ of crumbs in 9x13 pan. Fill with cheese mixture, then put remaining crumbs on top.

Cheesecake Tarts
Dena Hostetler

2 (8 oz.) pkg. cream cheese
1 c. sugar
⅓ c. Carnation milk
½ tsp. vanilla
3 eggs
vanilla wafers

Beat cream cheese and sugar together for 5 minutes; add milk and vanilla; add beaten eggs. Put 1 vanilla wafer on bottom of 24 cupcake papers, fill about ⅔ full. Bake at 350° approx. 20 minutes. When removed from oven the center will go down. Top with a spoonful of your favorite filling. Serves 24 people.

Cheese Tarts

Mrs. Marty (Esther) Miller

Crust:
2½ c. pastry flour
1 c. shortening (½ c. butter and
    ½ c. Crisco)
1 (8 oz.) pkg. cream cheese
pinch salt
Filling:
2 (8 oz.) pkg. cream cheese
1 c. white sugar
1 c. powdered sugar
2 eggs
2 Tbsp. butter, melted
1 tsp. vanilla
Topping:
pie filling of your choice

Mix crust ingredients like pie dough. Press dough in mini or regular muffin pans lined with paper cups. Top with cream cheese filling and your favorite pie filling. Bake at 350° for 15 minutes. Makes 54 mini tarts.

Rhubarb Custard Cake

Mrs. Kathryn Miller

1 yellow cake mix
5 c. diced rhubarb
1½-2 c. sugar
2 c. cream, not whipped, or
    1 can evaporated milk

Mix cake mix according to directions or you could make a basic yellow 2 egg cake from scratch. Pour cake mix into a 9x13 pan. Mix rhubarb and sugar together. I also add a few tablespoons strawberry gelatin. Pour over batter. Pour cream over all. Bake 45-55 minutes. The fruit and cream sink to the bottom and form a nice custard layer. Serves 10 people.

Frozen Peanut Butter Pudding

Mrs. Floyd (Mollie) Yoder

2 c. graham cracker crumbs
2 Tbsp. sugar
¼ c. butter, melted
1 (8 oz.) pkg. cream cheese
2 c. powdered sugar
⅔ c. peanut butter
1 c. milk
8 oz. Cool Whip
2 candy bars, chopped, optional

Combine cracker crumbs, sugar, and melted butter. Press into a 9x13 pan. Beat cream cheese till soft. Add powdered sugar and peanut butter; mix well. Slowly add milk, blending well. Pour on top of crackers. Freeze till solid. Top with Cool Whip. Garnish with chopped candy bars (if desired). Serves 15 people.

Frozen Chocolate Pudding

Loma Kauffman

2 c. graham cracker crumbs
⅓ c. butter
½ c. brown sugar
12 oz. cream cheese
1¾ c. sugar
⅔ c. cocoa
1⅓ c. milk
1 tsp. vanilla
32 oz. whipped cream

Combine graham cracker crumbs, sugar, and butter and press into 9x13 pan. Beat together rest of ingredients, adding whipped cream last. Put on top of graham cracker crust and freeze.

To soften brown sugar put in tight container. Add a piece of bread.

Fabulous Fruit Salad

Loma Kauffman

1 honeydew, cubed
1 cantaloupe, cubed
2 c. cubed seedless watermelon
2 peaches, peeled and cubed
2 nectarines, peeled and cubed
1 c. red seedless grapes
1 c. halved fresh strawberries
1 (11 oz.) can mandarin oranges,
  drained
2 kiwis, peeled, halved and sliced
2 firm bananas, sliced
1 lg. apple, cubed
1 can frozen lemonade concentrate,
  thawed
1 (3.4 oz.) pkg. instant vanilla pudding mix

In a large bowl combine the first nine ingredients. Cover and refrigerate for at least 1 hour. Just before serving stir in the bananas and apples. Combine lemonade concentrate and pudding mix. Pour over fruit and toss to coat.

Apple Crunch

Ella Yutzy

Top Part:
1 c. flour
1 c. brown sugar
¾ c. oatmeal
½ c. butter or margarine
1 Tbsp. cinnamon
4 c. diced apples
Filling:
2 Tbsp. cornstarch or Therm-Flo
1 c. sugar
1 c. water
1 tsp. vanilla

Mix the first five ingredients until crumbly. Press ½ of crumbs in a 9 inch baking dish. Cover with the diced apples; cook filling till clear and thick. Pour over apples. Cover with remaining crumbs. Bake at 350° for 1 hour.

Homemade Ice Cream

Faith Ann Yoder

2 boxes instant vanilla pudding
½ box instant butter pecan pudding
6 c. milk
4 eggs, separated
½ c. white sugar
¼ c. brown sugar
⅓ c. white Karo
½ tsp. vanilla
½ tsp. salt
1 can Eagle Brand milk

Mix pudding with 6 c. milk. Mix egg yolks, sugars, Karo, salt, and vanilla. Add Eagle Brand milk. Add all to stiffly beaten egg whites. Mix with instant pudding mixture and freeze. Makes 1 gallon.

Homemade Ice Cream

Mrs. Johnny (Ruby) Miller

6 c. whole milk
4 c. sugar
3 Tbsp. cornstarch
½ tsp. salt
5 eggs, separated
4 Tbsp. vanilla
1 (8 oz.) pkg. cream cheese
6 c. heavy cream

Heat 5 c. milk. Meanwhile, make a paste with 3 c. sugar, cornstarch, salt, egg yolks, and 1 c. milk. Stir into hot milk and bring to boil. Remove from heat; cream together softened cream cheese and 1 c. sugar; add to milk; add vanilla, cool. Add beaten egg whites and fill can with heavy cream to ¾ full. Leave space so ice cream can expand. Yield: 6 quarts.

Pies

Notes

Pumpkin Pie
Edith Engbretson

1 c. cooked pumpkin
½ c. sugar
½ c. brown sugar
1 Tbsp. flour
½ tsp. cinnamon
¼ tsp. cloves
¼ tsp. nutmeg
¼ tsp. salt
2 egg yolks
1 c. evaporated milk
2 egg whites

Mix first nine ingredients together, then add milk. Beat egg whites until thick, but not stiff. Fold into pumpkin mixture until well blended. Makes 1 pie. Bake at 425° for 10 minutes. Reduce temperature to 350° and bake until set.

Million-Dollar Pie
Mrs. David Kurtz

8 oz. Cool Whip
1 lg. can crushed pineapple
1 c. pecans or walnuts, crushed
1 can Eagle Brand milk, or
   any sweetened milk
¼ c. lemon juice

Mix all together and pour into pie shells. This is enough to make 2 pies at a time. Put in refrigerator. It also can be frozen. Eat when cold but not frozen. Can be put in graham cracker crust pie shell or a regular pie crust. A delicious and easy pie to make when you have extra pie crust left from making other pies.

Rhubarb Custard Pie
Emily Troyer

1½ c. sugar
2 Tbsp. flour
2 eggs
3 c. chopped rhubarb
 Crumbs:
½ c. flour
½ c. brown sugar
½ c. oatmeal
¼ c. butter

Mix sugar, flour, and beaten eggs and pour over rhubarb. Mix well and pour into crust. Melt butter and mix with rest of crumb mixture. Spread crumbs over batter and bake at 400° for 10 minutes, then at 350° until done.

Cream Pie

Emily Troyer

¾ c. sugar
¼ c. cornstarch
½ tsp. salt
4 egg yolks, beaten
2¾ c. milk
2 Tbsp. butter
1 Tbsp. vanilla
1 Tbsp. gelatin
¼ c. cold water
Cool Whip

Mix first three ingredients, then add milk and eggs. Cook until thick. Soak gelatin in water and add to boiling mixture. Remove from heat and add butter and vanilla. While cooling make sure you stir mixture often. Then add lots of Cool Whip before it gets too thick. You can put peanut butter crumbs, bananas, or coconut on pie, whatever you please.

Hershey Bar Pie

Edith Engbretson

17 marshmallows
¼ lb. butter
6 Hershey bars
½ pt. whipped cream
graham cracker crust

Melt marshmallows with butter. Add chocolate bars. Cool slightly. Add whipped cream. Pour in crust and chill.

Chocolate Shoofly Pie

Sarah Ann Miller

pastry for 9"single crust pie:
½ c. semisweet chocolate chips
1½ c. all-purpose flour
½ c. brown sugar, packed
3 Tbsp. butter
1 tsp. baking soda
1½ c. water
1 egg, beaten
1 c. molasses

Line a 9 inch deep-dish pie plate with pastry. Sprinkle chocolate chips into shell; set aside. In a large bowl, combine flour and brown sugar; cut in butter until crumbly. Set aside 1 cup for topping. Add baking soda, water, egg, and molasses to remaining crumb mixture; mix well. Pour over chips. Sprinkle with reserved crumb mixture. Bake at 350° for 45-55 minutes or until a knife inserted near the center comes out clean. Hint: You can use carob chips instead of chocolate chips for a healthier pie. Serves 6 to 8 people.

Caramel Custard Pie

Mrs. Steve (Linda) Kauffman

1 c. white sugar
1 Tbsp. flour, heaping
2 c. milk
2 eggs, separated
1 tsp. maple flavoring
pinch of salt

Mix flour, sugar, egg yolks, flavoring, and salt. Add enough milk to make a batter (from the 2 cups of milk). I like to use a cup of cream and a cup of milk. Bring milk to boiling point and add to other ingredients, then beat egg whites and fold in last. Sprinkle nuts on top. Bake at 375° for 10 minutes, then at 325° until done, approx. 40 minutes. Makes 1 pie.

Vanilla Cream Pudding

Lydiann Troyer

⅔ c. sugar
½ tsp. salt
3 Tbsp. cornstarch
3 c. milk
3 egg yolks
1 Tbsp. butter
cream cheese
1½ tsp. vanilla

Blend together sugar, salt, cornstarch, milk, and egg yolks. Boil over medium heat for 1 minute, stirring constantly. Remove from heat. Add butter, cream cheese, and vanilla. Whisk until smooth. Pour this into 4 baked pie shells and cool completely before you top with your favorite fruit filling and whipped topping. Delicious! Optional: You can use this as a basic pudding recipe for any pudding pies, omitting the cream cheese.

Pecan Pie

Ruth Bontrager

4 eggs, beaten well
½ c. white sugar
¼ tsp. salt
1 c. light corn syrup
¼ c. butter, melted
1 tsp. vanilla
1 c. pecan halves
1 pie shell, unbaked

Beat eggs well. Mix all ingredients except pecans in order given. Pour into unbaked pie shell. Place pecans on top of mixture. Bake at 400° for 10 minutes, then reduce to 350° until done.

Huckleberry Pie with Oatmeal Crust
Mrs. Kathryn Miller

32 lg. marshmallows
½ c. milk
2 c. cream, whipped
1 tsp. vanilla
½ c. sugar, or more to taste
2 c. huckleberries, heaping
  Oatmeal Crust:
1 c. quick-cooking oats
⅓ c. sifted flour
⅓ c. brown sugar
½ tsp. salt
⅓ c. butter

Melt marshmallows in top of double boiler with ½ c. milk. Cool, then mix with 2 c. cream, whipped with vanilla and sugar, or you can use Cool Whip. Mix in huckleberries. Put in 9 inch baked pie shell. I like a baked oatmeal crust. Mix together oats, flour, brown sugar, and salt, then cut in butter until crumbly. Press firmly in 9 inch pie pan. Bake in moderate oven 10-15 minutes. Do not overbake. Serves 6 to 8 people.

Huckleberry Pie
Laura Ann Miller

32 lg. marshmallows
½ c. milk
2 c. cream, whipped
1 tsp. vanilla
½ c. sugar
2 c. huckleberries, heaping
  Oatmeal Crust:
1 c. quick-cooking oats
⅓ c. sifted flour
⅓ c. brown sugar
½ tsp. salt
⅓ c. butter

Melt marshmallows in top of double boiler with ½ c. milk. Cool, then mix with 2 c. cream, whipped with vanilla and sugar. Mix in huckleberries. Pour into 2 small or 1 large oatmeal pie crust. *For Oatmeal Crust:* Mix together first four ingredients, then cut in butter until crumbly. Press firmly on bottom and sides of 9 inch pie plate. Bake at 350° for approx. 15 minutes. Do not overbake.

Cakes and Frostings

Notes

Cream-Filled Coffee Cake

Mrs. Julie Hochstetler

1 c. milk
½ c. butter
½ c. white sugar
1 tsp. salt
2 eggs
1 Tbsp. yeast
¼ c. warm water
3½ c. flour
  Crumbs:
½ c. flour
½ c. brown sugar
¼ c. butter
  Filling:
6 Tbsp. flour
½ c. white sugar
1½ c. milk
1 c. powdered sugar
1 c. Crisco
½ c. butter
1 tsp. vanilla
pinch of salt

Scald milk; add butter, sugar, and salt. Add beaten eggs. Add yeast dissolved in warm water. Mix in flour and let rise in refrigerator overnight. Cover dough with plastic wrap or foil. Next morning divide dough into 3 pie pans. Mix crumb ingredients and spread over dough and let rise. Bake at 350° for 15 minutes. Cool. Split each cake and fill with filling. *For Filling:* Cook flour, white sugar, and milk until thickened. Cool, then add powdered sugar, Crisco, butter, vanilla, and salt. Beat well.

Bundt Cake

Ruth Bontrager

1 box Duncan Hines yellow
  cake mix
1 box instant vanilla pudding, dry
1 c. milk
1 c. vegetable oil
4 eggs
1 (6 oz.) pkg. chocolate chips
1 German sweet chocolate bar,
  grated fine

Combine first five ingredients. Beat until blended, fold in chocolate chips and grated bar. Pour into well greased and floured Bundt pan. Bake at 350° for 50-60 minutes. Cool and remove from pan and sprinkle with powdered sugar.

Warm Winter Cake

Fannie Yoder

1 pkg. chocolate cake mix
2 c. cold milk
1¼ c. water
⅓ c. sugar
2 pkg. (4 serving size ea.) chocolate instant pudding
2 Tbsp. powdered sugar

Prepare cake mix according to directions. Pour in a greased 9x13 pan. Pour milk and water into a bowl, add dry pudding mixes and the ⅓ c. sugar. Beat with wire whip for 2 minutes or until well blended. Pour over cake batter. Bake 1 hour or until toothpick inserted comes out clean. Cool. Sprinkle with powdered sugar. Serve warm with ice cream.

Ho-Ho Cake

Esta Miller

1 chocolate cake mix
milk
butter
Ho-Ho Filling:
½ c. cream cheese
1 c. marshmallow creme
8 oz. Cool Whip
Chocolate Icing:
1½ c. brown sugar
¾ c. cream or evaporated milk
½ c. butter
1 c. chocolate chips

Mix cake mix with milk and butter instead of water and vegetable oil called for in cake mix. *Ho-Ho Filling:* Whip together softened cream cheese and marshmallow creme; add Cool Whip. *For Chocolate Icing:* Boil brown sugar and cream or evaporated milk together without stirring. Remove from heat; add butter and chocolate chips.

To cut a fresh cake, use a thin, sharp knife, dipped in water.

French Apple Crunch Cake

Mrs. David Kurtz

1½ c. vegetable oil
2 c. sugar
2 eggs
2 c. flour
1½ tsp. salt
1 tsp. baking soda
1 tsp. cinnamon
1 tsp. nutmeg
⅓ c. water
2 c. apples
1 tsp. vanilla
  Icing:
3 Tbsp. butter
3 Tbsp. milk
⅓ c. brown sugar
1 c. powdered sugar

Beat together first three ingredients, then mix in flour, salt, baking soda, cinnamon, and nutmeg; fold in water, apples, and vanilla. Bake at 350° for 35-45 minutes. *For Icing:* Melt butter; add brown sugar and milk. Bring to a boiling point; cool partly; add powdered sugar. Our favorite fall cake.

German Chocolate Cake

Dena Hostetler

½ c. water
4 oz. milk chocolate chips or solits
2 c. sugar
1 c. butter, shortening or margarine
4 eggs, separated
1 tsp. vanilla
1 tsp. soda
½ tsp. salt
2½ c. cake flour
1 c. buttermilk or sour milk

Heat water and chocolate in saucepan until melted. Beat sugar and butter until fluffy; beat in egg yolks. Blend in melted chocolate and vanilla. Combine dry ingredients. Add alternately with buttermilk. Beat until batter is smooth. Whip egg whites until stiff, fold into batter. Pour into 9x13 cake pan or your favorite pan. Bake at 350° for 30 minutes.

Icing for German Chocolate Cake

Dena Hostetler

1 can evaporated milk
4 egg yolks
½ c. butter
1½ c. sugar
1 lb. coconut
1½ c. nuts (pecans are best)
1 tsp. vanilla

In saucepan put milk and eggs, whip with wire whip. Add sugar and butter. Heat on low heat and stir until smooth and boiling; remove from heat and add coconut, nuts, and vanilla.

Amazin' Raisin Cake

Edith Engbretson

3 c. flour
2 c. sugar
1 c. mayonnaise
⅓ c. milk
2 eggs
2 tsp. baking soda
1½ tsp. cinnamon
½ tsp. nutmeg
½ tsp. salt
¼ tsp. cloves
3 c. chopped apples
1 c. raisins
½ c. chopped nuts

Stir together first ten ingredients. Then stir in apples, raisins, and nuts. Bake at 350° for 45 minutes. Frost with cream cheese frosting or eat with Cool Whip.

Caramel Cake

Mrs. Marty (Esther) Miller

1 cake mix, caramel, butter pecan,
  or chocolate
  First Layer:
1 (8 oz.) pkg. cream cheese
¾ c. topping, whipped
½ c. brown sugar
  Second Layer:
¾ c. brown sugar
¼ c. butter
½ c. sour cream

Mix cake as directed on package. Bake in cookie sheet. When cooled top with first layer. Mix second layer in saucepan and boil slowly for 5 minutes. Cool slightly, spread on first layer. Yummy!

Butter Pecan Cake
Brenda Beachy

1 butter pecan cake mix
1 (8 oz.) pkg. cream cheese
8 oz. Cool Whip
1 c. brown sugar
¼ c. butter, melted
¾ c. brown sugar
½ c. sour cream
1 Tbsp. milk

Bake cake mix as directed on package. Mix together cream cheese, Cool Whip, and brown sugar; spread on cooled cake. Boil together melted butter, brown sugar, sour cream, and milk for 3 minutes; when cooled spread on top of cream cheese layer.

Scotch Shortbread
Mrs. Amy Elizabeth Miller

1 c. butter, softened
½ c. brown sugar, packed
2 c. flour
¼ tsp. salt
¼ tsp. baking powder

Mix all ingredients together well till light and fluffy. Pack into a 9 inch round greased baking dish. Bake at 350° for 20-25 minutes (lightly browned). Let set for 5 minutes before taking out of pan. Very good with any fresh fruit.

Caramel Roll-Me-Ups
Fannie Yoder

2 cans jumbo biscuits
Topping:
1 c. brown sugar
4 Tbsp. butter, melted
½ c. maple or pancake syrup
½ c. nuts
Filling:
1 (8 oz.) pkg. cream cheese
2 Tbsp. butter, softened
¼ c. powdered sugar

Mix topping and place in bottom of a 9x13 pan. Combine filling ingredients and mix well. Flatten biscuits into oval shape. Place 1 Tbsp. cream cheese filling on center of biscuits and roll to make sausage shaped and pinch seam closed. Place in baking dish, seam side down. Bake at 375° for approx. 45 minutes, until nicely browned, and invert on platter to serve.

Chocolate Torte

Mrs. Jeremy (Rose) Miller

1 c. butter, softened
2½ c. sugar
4 eggs
1½ tsp. vanilla
1 c. cocoa
2 c. boiling water
2¾ c. all-purpose flour
2 tsp. soda
½ tsp. baking powder
½ tsp. salt
  Filling:
1 c. heavy whipping cream
¼ c. powdered sugar
1 tsp. vanilla
  Frosting:
1 c. semisweet chocolate chips
1 c. butter, cubed
½ c. heavy whipping cream
2½ c. powdered sugar

In a large mixing bowl, cream butter and sugar. Add eggs, one at a time, beating well after each addition. Add vanilla. Whisk cocoa and water until smooth. Combine dry ingredients; add to creamed mixture alternately with cocoa mixture. Beat until smooth. Pour into 3 greased and floured 9 inch round baking pans. Bake at 350° about 25 minutes. Cool for 10 minutes; remove from pans to wire racks. In a mixing bowl, beat cream, powdered sugar, and vanilla on high speed until soft peaks form. Chill until firm. In a saucepan, melt chocolate chips and butter over medium heat; stir in cream. Remove from heat; stir in powdered sugar. Chill at least 1 hour or until completely cooled. Beat with electric mixer to achieve spreading consistency. Spread half of the filling over 1 cake layer; top with second layer and remaining filling. Top with third layer; frost top and sides of cake. Chill for 2 hours before cutting. Serves 12 people.

Easy Cake Mix Rolls

Emily Troyer

2 Tbsp. yeast
1 yellow cake mix
4½ c. flour
2½ c. warm water

Mix yeast and water. Add cake mix and flour. Let rise until double in bulk. Roll out dough and spread with butter, cinnamon, and brown sugar. Roll in rolls, cut in slices. Let rise in pans and bake 20 minutes. Delicious if frosted with cream cheese frosting.

Coffee Cake or Bars
Sarah Ann Miller

1½ c. sugar
½ c. butter
2 eggs
1 c. milk
3 c. flour
1½ tsp. baking powder
1 tsp. salt
  Topping:
1 c. brown sugar
4 Tbsp. flour
4 Tbsp. butter, melted
4 Tbsp. water
4 tsp. cinnamon

Mix sugar, butter, and eggs well. Add dry ingredients alternately with milk. Spread ½ of batter on greased cookie sheet. Mix together topping ingredients and sprinkle half on batter. Spread on the rest of the batter, then the remaining topping. Circle with a fork for a marbled effect. Bake at 350° for 20-25 minutes, cut in squares and drizzle with icing.

Jelly Roll Cake
Sarah Ann Miller

4 eggs, separated
¾ c. sugar
1 tsp. vanilla
⅔ c. sifted cake flour
¼ tsp. salt
1 tsp. baking powder
  Jelly Roll Filling:
4 oz. cream cheese, softened
1 c. powdered sugar
1 c. strawberries, well-strained
8 oz. Cool Whip

Beat egg whites until soft peaks form. Gradually add sugar and beat until stiff peaks form. Beat egg yolks and add vanilla. Fold yolks into whites. Sift together dry ingredients and fold in mixture. Grease bottom of jelly roll pan and put on wax paper and grease wax paper on top. Pour batter into greased pan and bake at 375° for 10-12 minutes. Remove from pan onto towel sprinkled with powdered sugar. Roll and cool. Mix together cream cheese, powdered sugar, and strawberries. Fold in Cool Whip. When roll has cooled, unroll and spread with filling, then roll again. Slice and serve.

Pumpkin Roll
Dena Hostetler

3 egg yolks
¾ c. pumpkin
1 c. sugar
1 c. cake flour
1 tsp. baking powder
½ tsp. cinnamon
¼ tsp. ginger
¼ tsp. salt
egg whites, beaten
1 tsp. cream of tartar
 Filling:
1 (8 oz.) pkg. cream cheese
2 c. powdered sugar

Mix together all ingredients, except egg whites and cream of tartar. Beat egg whites with cream of tartar, and add to batter; mix until egg whites are well mixed in. Pour into 13x18 cookie sheet or 2 jelly roll pans lined with wax paper. Bake at 350° for about 10 minutes or if batter won't fall when touched. Spread powdered sugar over top and put paper towel or cheesecloth on top. Flip over and roll up until cool, then unroll and spread with filling. Roll up again.

Cocoa Icing
Mrs. Steve (Linda) Kauffman

1 c. white sugar
4 Tbsp. cocoa
2 Tbsp. cornstarch
1 c. boiling water

Boil till thick, then add 2 Tbsp. butter and vanilla.

Cream Cheese Frosting
Emily Troyer

1 (8 oz.) pkg. cream cheese
½ c. butter
1 tsp. vanilla
2 c. powdered sugar

Cream cream cheese and butter. Add rest of ingredients. Very delicious and simple.

Cookies

and Bars

Notes

Peanut Butter Blossoms

Mrs. Sheila Schrock

2 c. margarine plus ½ c. Crisco
3 c. brown sugar
3 c. white sugar
3 c. peanut butter
6 eggs
1½ tsp. salt
⅛ c. baking soda
3 tsp. baking powder
3 tsp. vanilla
6 c. oatmeal
5 c. flour
M&M's

Mix together in order listed. Bake at 350°.

Potato Butterscotch Chip Cookies

Mrs. Floyd (Mollie) Yoder

1 c. shortening
½ c. white sugar
1 c. brown sugar
2 eggs
2 tsp. vanilla
2 c. plus 4 Tbsp. flour
1 tsp. baking powder
½ tsp. salt
2 c. crushed potato chips
1 (8 oz.) pkg. butterscotch chips

Cream shortening and sugar in medium size bowl. Add eggs and vanilla. Combine flour, baking powder, and salt. Add to egg mixture. Stir in crushed potato chips and butterscotch chips. Make dough into walnut sized balls on cookie sheets, 2 inches apart, flatten with fork. Bake at 350° for 8-10 minutes. Yield: 3 dozen.

I got this recipe from my paternal grandmother. She was 88 years old at the time and still baking cookies to sell.

Sugar-Free Cookies

Dena Hostetler

2 c. raisins
2 c. dates, chopped
2 c. water
1 c. butter
4 eggs
1 tsp. vanilla
2 tsp. soda
1 tsp. cinnamon
1 c. whole wheat flour
1½-2 c. white flour

Cook raisins, dates, and water together for a few minutes. In mixer beat butter, eggs, and vanilla; add dates and raisins. Mix and add rest of ingredients. Drop on cookie sheets and bake at 350° for 5-10 minutes. Makes approx. 4½ dozen.

Rice Krispie Cookies

Amy Engbretson

1 c. white sugar
1 c. brown sugar
1 c. peanut butter
1 c. butter
2 eggs
1 tsp. soda
1 tsp. baking powder
8 c. Rice Krispies
12 oz. semisweet chocolate chips

Mix together in medium bowl. Bake at 325° for 10-12 minutes. Cool on pan for 5 minutes before removing from pan.

Hair spray removes ink from clothing.

Healthy Pumpkin Whoopie Cookies

Mrs. Nancy Troyer

1½ c. Sucanat or fructose
2 c. pumpkin
1 c. butter
1 tsp. vanilla
2 eggs
3 c. speltz
2½ tsp. cinnamon
1 tsp. cloves
1 tsp. soda
2 tsp. baking powder
1 tsp. salt
2 c. carob chips
  Filling:
5 Tbsp. flour
1¼ c. milk
½ c. butter
1 c. Crisco
¾ c. sugar or fructose

Cream together sweetener and butter. Beat in pumpkin, vanilla, and eggs; add spices, baking powder, and soda, then add speltz. Mix well. Add carob chips. These are very good. Bake at 350°. *To Make Filling:* Mix flour and milk and put in saucepan, cook till thick. Cool. Beat in butter, sugar, and Crisco.

Simple and Delicious Chocolate Whoopie Pies

Dena Hostetler

4 c. sugar
8 c. cake flour
2 c. cocoa powder
4 tsp. soda
1 tsp. salt
2 tsp. vanilla
⅓ c. vinegar
3½ c. water
1½ c. vegetable oil
  Icing or Filling:
⅔ c. milk
⅔ c. flour
3 c. Crisco
1 tsp. vanilla
6 c. powdered sugar

Mix together dry ingredients with wire whip, then add the wet ingredients. Cake flour makes the best cookies, but other flour works as well. After all ingredients are together whip until smooth, add more or less flour or water to get texture perfect. This is a large batch that I use in my bakery. One batch makes around 55 sandwiches. You might want to cut it in half. *For Icing or Filling:* Cook together milk and flour until thick. Cool a little and add Crisco, vanilla and powdered sugar, more or less. Whip together.

Christmas Cutout Cookies
Mrs. Steve (Linda) Kauffman

2 eggs
1½ c. white sugar
1 c. butter, softened
1 c. sweet milk
1 tsp. vanilla
4 c. flour
2 tsp. baking powder
2 tsp. cream of tartar
2 tsp. soda
 Frosting:
¼ c. butter
1¾ c. powdered sugar
1 egg
1 tsp. vanilla

Cream butter, sugar, and eggs. Add to batter alternately with milk, vanilla, and dry ingredients. Let it set in a cold place for 10-15 minutes before rolling out dough.

Outrageous Chocolate Chip Cookies
Fannie Yoder

1 c. butter flavored Crisco
1 c. sugar
2 eggs
2 c. flour
2 tsp. soda
1 c. peanut butter
⅔ c. brown sugar
1 tsp. vanilla
1 c. rolled oats
½ tsp. salt
2 c. chocolate chips

Cream Crisco, peanut butter, and sugars. Add eggs and vanilla. Combine flour, oats, soda, and salt; mix well. Stir in chocolate chips. Drop by teaspoon on ungreased cookie sheet. Bake at 350° for 10-12 minutes or until lightly browned.

Favorite Chocolate Chip Cookies

Rachel Troyer

½ c. margarine
½ c. white sugar
¾ c. brown sugar
½ c. vegetable oil
2 eggs
1½ tsp. baking soda
1 tsp. salt
1 tsp. vanilla
⅔ c. instant vanilla pudding
3 c. all-purpose flour
2 c. semisweet chocolate chips
nuts, optional

Cream together margarine and sugars. Add all other ingredients except chocolate chips and nuts. Mix well. Add chocolate chips and nuts. Bake at 350° for 10-12 minutes. Yield: approx. 3 doz.

Chocolate Chip Cookies

Rebecca Kurtz (age 11)

1 c. butter or margarine
1 c. peanut butter
1 c. white sugar
⅔ c. brown sugar, packed
2 eggs
1 tsp. vanilla
2 c. all-purpose flour
1 c. oatmeal
2 tsp. baking soda
½ tsp. salt
⅔ c. cinnamon drops
⅔ c. milk chocolate drops
⅔ c. peanut butter drops
⅔ c. butterscotch drops
⅔ c. semisweet drops

Cream butter, peanut butter, and sugars. Add eggs, one at a time, stirring after each egg. Beat in vanilla, soda, salt, flour, and oats. Stir in chips last. Bake at 350° for 10 minutes. Our favorite chocolate chip cookies.

Moist Chocolate Chip Cookies
Emily Troyer

1½ c. butter
1⅛ c. brown sugar
⅔ c. white sugar
1 c. instant pudding
3 eggs
1½ tsp. soda
5¼ c. quick oats
2 c. chocolate chips
1¼ c. flour

Mix first five ingredients well. Stir in remaining ingredients; mix well. Bake at 350° until brown. Do not overbake!

Golden Peanut Butter Bars
Mrs. Amy Miller

2 c. flour
¾ c. brown sugar, packed
1 egg, beaten
½ c. butter
1 (14 oz.) can sweetened
  condensed milk
½ c. peanut butter
1 tsp. vanilla
½ c. chocolate chips

Preheat oven to 350°. Combine flour, sugar, and egg in large bowl. Cut in cold butter until crumbly. Reserve 2 c. crumb mixture. Press remaining mixture in bottom of 9x13 pan. Bake 15 minutes or until lightly browned. Meanwhile, beat sweetened condensed milk, peanut butter, and vanilla in another bowl. Spread over prepared crust. Sprinkle chocolate chips over filling, then top with reserved crumb mixture. Bake an additional 15-20 minutes or until lightly browned.

Reese's Cake Squares
Fannie Yoder

1 c. butter
4 Tbsp. cocoa
1 c. water
2 c. flour
2 c. sugar
1 tsp. baking powder
2 eggs
1 tsp. vanilla
  Glaze:
1 c. chocolate chips
4 Tbsp. butter
2 Tbsp. light corn syrup

Bring butter, cocoa, and water to a boil. Pour over dry ingredients. Add eggs and vanilla. Pour into greased 10x15 cookie sheet. Bake at 350° for 30 minutes (or when inserted toothpick comes out clean). When cooled spread a layer of peanut butter on top. Top with chocolate chip glaze. *For Glaze:* Combine ingredients in saucepan. Put on low heat. Stir constantly until melted. Cool slightly.

Raisin Puffs
Miriam Schlabach

1 c. water
1½ c. raisins
3½ c. flour
1 tsp. baking soda
½ tsp. salt
1½ c. sugar
1 c. margarine or butter, softened
2 eggs
1 tsp. vanilla
½ c. sugar
1 tsp. cinnamon

Boil water in a saucepan. Add the raisins and boil until the water is gone; cool. Combine the flour, soda, and salt. Beat together 1½ c. sugar and margarine or butter until combined. Add eggs and vanilla; beat well. Add the dry ingredients to the beaten mixture; beat until blended. Stir in raisins. Combine ½ c. sugar and cinnamon. Shape dough into 1 inch balls; roll in cinnamon sugar. Place 2 inches apart on ungreased cookie sheets. Bake at 375° for 8 minutes. Yield: 70 raisin puffs.

Raisin Bars

Crust:
1 c. butter, melted
1 c. brown sugar
2 c. quick oatmeal
1½ c. flour
1 tsp. soda

Raisin Mixture:
1 c. raisins
1¼ c. sour cream
¾ c. sugar
¼ c. flour
2 Tbsp. lemon juice
1 tsp. vanilla
1 egg

Boil raisins for 5 minutes, then drain off water. Set aside. Mix crust ingredients and press half into a greased 9x13 pan. Bake at 350° for 10 minutes. Meanwhile, mix all the raisin mixture ingredients together. Pour over baked crust; add the rest of the crust mixture on top and bake an additional 30 minutes.

Chocolate Chip Toffee Bars
Mary L. Troyer

2½ c. flour
⅔ c. brown sugar
¾ c. butter or margarine
1 egg, slightly beaten
2 c. semisweet chocolate chips, divided
1 c. nuts, chopped
1 can sweetened condensed milk
1¾ c. English toffee bits, divided

Preheat oven to 350°. Grease a 13x9x2 baking pan. In a large bowl stir together flour and brown sugar. Cut in butter until mixture resembles coarse crumbs. Add egg; mix well. Stir in 1½ c. chocolate chips and nuts. Reserve 1½ c. mixture. Press remaining crumb mixture into bottom of prepared pan. Bake 10 minutes. Pour sweetened condensed milk over hot crust. Top with 1½ c. toffee bits. Sprinkle reserved crumb mixture and remaining ½ c. chips over top. Bake 25-30 minutes. Sprinkle with remaining ¼ c. toffee bits. Cut while still warm. Yield: 36 bars.

Toffee Walnut Bars

Mrs. Amy Elizabeth Miller

1 c. butter
1 c. brown sugar
1 egg
1 tsp. vanilla
2 c. flour
1½ c. chocolate chips
½ c. walnuts

Cream together butter and brown sugar. Add egg, vanilla, and flour. Spread in an ungreased 9x13 pan and bake at 350° for 12-15 minutes. Sprinkle chocolate chips on the hot bars, then spread even once they are melted. Sprinkle chopped walnuts on top. They are fun, fast, and full of flavor.

Date Squares

Sarah Ann Miller

Crumbs:
2 c. oatmeal
2 c. wheat flour
1 c. butter
½ c. honey
½ tsp. salt
Filling:
3 c. dates
½ c. honey
1 tsp. vanilla
water to cover

Cook filling till well thickened. Set aside to cool. Mix crumbs. Press ¾ of crumbs into bottom of 9x13 pan. Spread filling on top of crumbs. Sprinkle remaining crumbs on top. Bake at 350° for 25-30 minutes or until nicely browned. Note: 1½ quart well thickened and sweetened cooked fruit may be used instead of dates.

Crunch Bars

½ c. butter
¾ c. sugar
2 eggs
1 tsp. vanilla
¾ c. flour
¼ tsp. baking powder
¼ tsp. salt
Topping:
1 c. chocolate chips
1 c. peanut butter
1½ c. Rice Krispies

Cream butter and sugar; beat in eggs and rest of ingredients. Bake in a cake pan at 350° for 20 minutes. Remove from oven and put 2½ c. miniature marshmallows on top. Return to oven 3 minutes till marshmallows are melted. Allow to cool 30 minutes. *To Make Topping:* Melt chocolate chips and peanut butter. Add Rice Krispies. Spread on top of bars. A good picnic bar.

Cherry Squares

1 c. butter
1 tsp. vanilla
2 eggs
2 c. sugar
1 tsp. almond or vanilla flavoring
3 c. flour
1 tsp. baking powder
1 can cherry pie filling

In a medium sized bowl, cream butter and sugar. Add flavoring. Beat in eggs, one at a time. Add flour and baking powder. Mix well. Press half of dough into a jelly roll pan. Spread pie filling on top of it. Top with remaining dough. Bake at 350° for 45 minutes. Cool. Cut in 2½ inch squares. Yield: 2 dozen squares. I use other pie fillings too. Apple, raspberry, blueberry, and strawberry work well.

Chocolate Zucchini Bars

Edith Engbretson

4 eggs
1½ c. vegetable oil
2 c. sugar
2 c. flour
2 tsp. baking soda
2 tsp. cinnamon
1 tsp. salt
4 Tbsp. cocoa
1 tsp. vanilla
3 c. grated zucchini
 Frosting:
3 oz. cream cheese
½ c. butter, softened
2 c. powdered sugar
2 Tbsp. cocoa
1 tsp. vanilla

Mix eggs, vegetable oil, and sugar. Next add dry ingredients. Last add zucchini. Put in cookie sheet and bake at 350° for 20-30 minutes. Spread frosting over bars.

Spicy Chocolate Bars

Faith Ann Yoder

1½ c. shortening
1½ c. sugar
1½ c. brown sugar
4 eggs
2 tsp. vanilla
4 c. flour
2 tsp. soda
2 tsp. salt
4 tsp. cinnamon
1 tsp. cloves
1 tsp. nutmeg
chocolate chips

Cream shortening and sugar together, then add rest of ingredients in order given. Bake at 375° for 20 minutes in an ungreased 12x16 pan.

Double-Deck Brownies

Laura Ann Miller

Bottom Layer:
2 c. flour
1 tsp. soda
1 tsp. salt
4 c. rolled oats
2 c. brown sugar
2 c. butter, melted
Top Layer:
3 c. sugar
4 eggs
1 c. butter, melted
¾ c. cocoa
1 tsp. baking powder
1 tsp. salt
2 tsp. vanilla
2¾ c. flour
1 c. milk

24 oz. chocolate chips
1½ c. peanut butter

Mix bottom layer ingredients and press into 2 jelly roll pans. Bake at 350° for 5-10 minutes. Mix top layer ingredients. Pour on bottom layer. Bake at 350° till done. Do not overbake. Melt chocolate chips; add peanut butter and spread on top.

Tips and Hints

To heat large roasters of casseroles, etc. for a 6:00 supper, put in 200° oven at 1:30. It will heat evenly and not have a burned top and roaster. No need to check and stir every 15 minutes either.

Since boiled potatoes turn out mushy when defrosted, they do not freeze well. But you can freeze potatoes if you bake them first. They keep a much nicer texture and can be used in cooked dishes such as stews, soups, and casseroles. They are delicious fried, too.

Blanch - Green string beans in boiling water, for 3 minutes.
Blanch - Peas in boiling water for 1½ minutes.
Blanch - Carrots in boiling water for 3 minutes. Cool immediately after removing from boiling water. Leave ½ inch head space, then freeze. It takes the same amount of time to cool veggies as it did to blanch them.

To remove pine pitch from clothing, place fabric between 2 facial tissues. Iron with a warm iron. Spray with Simple Green. Rub well with a soft cloth. Wash by hand, with warm water and detergent. Rinse dry. Repeat till pitch is gone.

If you want to make scrambled eggs for breakfast while on a hunting or camping trip, prepare it beforehand. Beat the amount of eggs you'll need. Pour it into an empty pop bottle. Pack it in with any frozen foods.

Smoothies and Beverages

Notes

Tropical Peach Smoothie

Mrs. Julie Hochstetler

3 c. frozen peaches
1 c. crushed pineapple
½ c. frozen orange juice
    concentrate
2 tsp. lemon juice
½ c. coconut, optional
sweetener to taste

Put in blender and add approx. 3 c. water. Blend until smooth. Serves 4 to 6 people.

Mission Mountain Margarita Shakes

Mrs. Jerry Miller

vanilla ice cream
Mountain Dew
Margarita mix

Fill blender with ice cream. Add ¾ c. Margarita mix and enough Mountain Dew to make the right consistency. Blend well. Delicious!

Peach Smoothie

Mrs. Jerry Miller

2 c. milk
2 c. frozen peaches
¼ c. orange juice concentrate
5 ice cubes
1 banana, optional

In a blender, combine all ingredients. Cover and process until smooth. Serve immediately. Serves 4 people.

Orange Julius

Lorene Yoder

1 (6 oz.) can frozen orange juice
    concentrate
1 c. milk
1 c. water
¼ c. sugar
1 tsp. vanilla extract
10-12 ice cubes

In a blender, combine orange juice concentrate, milk, water, sugar, and vanilla. Cover and blend well. With blender running, add ice cubes one at a time. Blend till smooth. Serve immediately. Very refreshing and tasty. Serves 4 to 5 people.

Good Luck Punch

Mrs. Steve (Linda) Kauffman

1 qt. rhubarb, about 2 doz. stalks
3 c. sugar
2 c. water
juice of 6 lemons
1 c. pineapple juice
1 qt. ginger ale

Cut rhubarb coarsely; add water to cover. Cook until soft, about 10 minutes. Drain. You should have approx. 3 quarts juice. Dissolve sugar in 2 c. water. Cook 10 minutes to make a syrup. Add lemon, pineapple and rhubarb juice. Pour over a chunk of ice in punch bowl. Just before serving add ginger ale. Makes 1 gallon punch.

Cocoa Mix

Fannie Yoder

8 qt. box dry milk
2 lb. Nesquik
1 lb. powdered sugar
16 oz. jar Coffee Mate
    powdered creamer

Mix together. To serve: Add ⅓ c. mix to 1 c. hot water.

Wassail

Mary L. Troyer

8 qt. water
4 c. sugar
2 tsp. cloves
1 tsp. butter
1 (12 oz.) can frozen orange juice
    concentrate
1 (12 oz.) can frozen lemonade
    concentrate
1 (46 oz.) can pineapple juice
1 (64 oz.) can cranberry juice

Bring water, sugar, cloves, and butter to a boil, then add rest of ingredients. A good drink after a skating party. Serve warm.

Amy's Sparkling Grape Juice

Mrs. Amy Miller

1 gal. red grape juice
1 (2 lt.) bottle ginger ale

Mix together and add ice. Very refreshing.

Basic Herb Syrup or Tea

Mrs. Kathryn Miller

3 c. water
1 c. fresh garden tea
2 c. sugar

Bring water to a boil and pour over tea. Cover and infuse for several hours. Strain and combine liquid with the sugar in a non-aluminum saucepan and cook, stirring occasionally, until the syrup thickens, approx. 10 minutes. Remove from heat. Cool and can or bottle. Will keep in refrigerator 3 months or cold pack 10 minutes. Add ¼ c. or less to a glass of water or pour over ice.

Iced Coffee Syrup

3¼ c. boiling water
1 c. instant coffee
   (I use Taster's Choice)
½ c. vanilla syrup
¼ c. caramel syrup
1½ c. white sugar

Use ⅓ c. syrup in tall kitchen glass; add milk and chopped ice. Optional: Top with whipped cream and drizzle with caramel topping (sundae). Refreshing on a warm summer day.

"The devil is forever busy convincing the people of other people's sins. The Holy Spirit convicts us of our own."

Russian Tea

Amy Engbretson

4 Tbsp. mint leaves
½ c. sugar
10 whole cloves
3 sticks cinnamon
½ gal. boiling water
juice of 2 oranges
juice of ½ lemon

Pour boiling water over tea, sugar, cinnamon, and cloves. Steep for 10 minutes. Strain and add fruit juices. Serve hot or cold. Serves 8 people.

Strawberry Lemonade

1½ c. strawberries
1 c. fresh lemon juice, approx. 6 lemons
1¼ c. sugar (can reduce)
4 c. cold water
ice cubes

Combine strawberries, lemon juice, and sugar in blender until smooth. Pour into large pitcher and add water, ice cubes, and lemon slices. Yield: 7 cups. Serves 7 people.

Frozen Tea Concentrate

Amy Engbretson

4 qt. water
2 qt. tightly packed tea leaves
3 c. white sugar

Bring water to a boil and remove from heat. Add tea and sugar. Let set for 1 hour. Strain. Cool. Put in 1 quart freezer container. When ready to serve, add 3 parts water to 1 part tea.

Eggnog (without raw eggs)
Dena Hostetler

4 c. whole milk
¼ c. instant vanilla pudding
¼ c. sugar
1 tsp. vanilla
1 tsp. cinnamon
¼ tsp. nutmeg
pinch of salt, optional
2 c. milk, or more

Put 4 c. milk in blender, or a beater works as well; add sugar and all the rest of ingredients except milk. Let set for 15 minutes. Stir once or twice until spices don't settle anymore; add 2 more cups of milk. Mix well and refrigerate for a while or serve whenever you wish. Serves 6 people.

Iced Coffee
Amy Engbretson

1 c. sugar
3 Tbsp. instant coffee
3 c. strong brewed coffee
1 tsp. vanilla
milk
ice

Mix sugar, instant coffee, brewed coffee, and vanilla in a gallon pitcher. Stir until sugar is dissolved. Add milk until ½ full. Fill with ice. Stir.

Mocha Punch
Amy Engbretson

½ c. Nesquik
1½ qt. water
½ c. sugar
¼ c. instant coffee

Heat water and rest of ingredients. Stir till heated. Cool completely. Thirty minutes before serving pour into punch bowl and add 1 gallon ice cream dipped into balls; ½ vanilla and ½ coffee ice cream is delicious. Garnish with whipped cream and chocolate curls.

Frosty Cantaloupe Sipper
Loma Kauffman

2 c. cubed cantaloupe
1 c. orange juice
1 Tbsp. sugar
1 Tbsp. lemon juice

Freeze cantaloupe cubes in a shallow pan for 1 hour or till firm. In a blender container combine cantaloupe, orange juice, sugar, and lemon juice. Cover and blend until smooth. Serves 3 people.

Our Favorite Sherbet Drink
Mrs. David (Katie) Kurtz

1 qt. orange sherbet
1 qt. vanilla ice cream
1 qt. ginger ale
2 cans frozen orange juice
concentrate

Combine sherbet, ice cream, and orange juice; add ginger ale last. Good for birthday parties! Serves 8 to 12 people.

Frosties
Mrs. Sheila Schrock

6 c. hot water
½ c. Nesquik chocolate powder
½ c. white sugar
¼ c. instant coffee
½ gal. vanilla ice cream

Heat first four ingredients to boiling and stir until dissolved. Cool and refrigerate. When ready to serve, pour over softened ice cream and mix well. Serve in glasses with straws and spoons. Serves 10 people.

All the fine praise, all the good wishes, will never replace—help with the dishes!

Notes

Blueberry or Huckleberry Pie Filling
Mrs. Jeremy (Rose) Miller

10 c. cold water
3 Tbsp. lemon juice
1½ c. instant clear jel
4 c. sugar
1 tsp. salt

Put water and lemon juice in Fix and Mix bowl. Mix dry ingredients together, then use whisk to stir water while slowly adding dry ingredients. I use 3 c. fructose instead of the sugar. Fill bowl about ¾ full with blueberries or huckleberries. Put in jars and cold pack for 20 minutes. Makes 4 quarts. So simple to make and very good on cheesecake, pancakes, French toast, etc.

Blueberry Pie Filling
Mrs. Johnny (Ruby) Miller

14 qt. water
39 c. sugar
pinch of salt
13 c. Therm-Flo
13 c. cold water
½ c. vanilla
3⅓ c. blueberry Jell-O
1 c. lemon juice
8 pks. berry blue Kool-Aid
3 gal. frozen blueberries, approx.

Bring 14 quarts water to boil; add sugar and salt. Mix 13 c. Therm-Flo with 13 c. cold water. Stir into boiling sugar water. Remove from heat. Add vanilla, Jell-O, Kool-Aid, lemon juice, and blueberries. Enough for 50 pies. For cherry pie use cherry Jell-O and cherry Kool-Aid. This is what we use for our auction pies.

Canned Peach Glaze
Mrs. Floyd (Mollie) Yoder

6 qt. peaches, peeled and sliced
3 c. water
3 c. orange juice or pineapple juice
7 c. sugar
1¾ c. Perma-Flo
1¾ c. water

In a 6 quart saucepan, heat water, juice, and sugar. Bring to a boil. In a mixing bowl stir together the Perma-Flo and water. Slowly stir into boiling syrup. Let boil, stirring constantly, till thickened. Add peaches. Fill quart jars only to neck. Cold pack 20 minutes. (A half bushel peaches makes a double batch and yields 14 quarts.) We use this as a glaze on cake with cream cheese filling, or serve it just as a thickened fruit.

Zucchini Orange Jam
Ruth Bontrager

6 c. shredded zucchini
6 c. sugar
2 Tbsp. lemon juice
1 (8 oz.) can crushed pineapple
   with juice
2 (3 oz.) pkg. orange Jell-O

In a large saucepan, combine zucchini, sugar, lemon juice, and pineapple with juice. Bring to a boil. Cook, stirring often, at a full boil for 10 minutes. Remove from heat. Stir in Jell-O. Spoon into jars. Cover and seal. Let cool. Can also be put in freezer. Makes 7 (½ pint) jars.

Grape Jelly

1 gal. Concord grapes
1 c. water
3 c. sugar

Wash and strain grapes. Put in saucepan and add water. Cook 20 minutes. Take 2 c. of this juice and bring to boil. Add sugar. Boil 1 minute. Ladle quickly into jars and seal. Will thicken to jelly consistency.

Peach Stone Jelly
Mrs. Kathryn Miller

peach pits
5 c. juice
1 pkg. Sure-Jell
5 c. sugar

Put the pits in a pan, cover to simmer 20 minutes or so. Strain the juice. Measure out 5 c. liquid, put on burner to boil with the package of Sure-Jell. When a full rolling boil is reached, add the sugar and boil until jelly stage. A good way to test is using an ordinary table fork and if liquid clings between tines it is done. This sometimes takes quite a while. Pour in jelly jars and seal. Very good and so attractive. Save the pits when you are canning or freezing peaches. The redder the pits, the better. I like the Red Havens.

Zucchini Relish
Ruth Bontrager

5 c. unpeeled ground zucchini
3 c. ground celery
3 c. ground onion
¾ c. ground pepper
6 c. water
¼ c. salt
3 c. white vinegar
6 c. sugar
2 Tbsp. mustard seed
1 tsp. turmeric
1 tsp. celery seed

Mix first six ingredients. Let set 1 hour. Drain and add next five ingredients. Cook together 10 minutes. Fill jars with hot relish and seal.

Hot Dog Relish
Arlene Bontrager

4 c. onions, chopped
12 green peppers, chopped
4 c. cabbage, chopped
10 green tomatoes, chopped
½ c. salt
4 c. vinegar
2 c. water
2 Tbsp. mustard seed
1 Tbsp. celery seed
1½ Tbsp. turmeric
6 c. sugar
½ c. clear jel

Sprinkle salt over chopped vegetables, let set overnight. Next morning, drain and rinse and drain again. Combine vinegar, water, mustard seed, celery seed, turmeric, and sugar. Mix with vegetables and bring to a boil. Boil 5-10 minutes. Thicken with clear jel in a little water. Put in hot jars and seal. This is good on sandwiches and also to make tartar sauce, by using half relish and half salad dressing, plus a little mustard.

Delicious Salsa

Ella Yutzy

14 c. chopped tomatoes, unpeeled
3 c. onions
½ c. jalapeno peppers
1 c. green peppers
½ c. vinegar
½ c. tomato sauce
3 Tbsp. salt
1 Tbsp. chili powder
1 Tbsp. garlic powder
1½ tsp. cumin
5 Tbsp. clear jel

Chop tomatoes, onions, and peppers and put in a saucepan, add remaining ingredients except clear jel and bring to a boil. Mix clear jel with water; add slowly and bring to boil. Put in jars and cold pack 10 minutes. Yield: approx. 10 pints.

Pizza Sauce

Mrs. David (Katie) Kurtz

½ bushel tomatoes or
   8 qt. juice
3 lb. onions
4 hot peppers
2 c. cooking oil
1 Tbsp. basil
3 Tbsp. oregano
1 c. sugar
½ c. salt
2 (18 oz.) cans tomato paste

Cook tomatoes to soup stage, 2½ to 3 hours. Grind onions and hot peppers and brown in cooking oil. Add to tomato juice. Then add basil, oregano, sugar, and salt. Cook another hour. Add tomato paste. Bring to a boil. Pack in hot jars and seal. Yield: 20 pints.

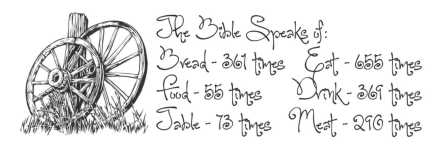

The Bible Speaks of:
Bread - 361 times   Eat - 655 times
Food - 55 times   Drink - 369 times
Table - 73 times   Meat - 296 times

Pizza Sauce

Amy Engbretson

1 gal. tomato paste
9 qt. tomato juice
3 Tbsp. chili powder
6 Tbsp. salt
9 Tbsp. parsley flakes
6 Tbsp. paprika
3 Tbsp. oregano
3 Tbsp. garlic powder
3 Tbsp. dry mustard
2 Tbsp. pepper
3 c. white sugar
1 qt. ketchup
8 green peppers or celery ribs
9 onions
2¼ c. Parmesan cheese

Drain tomato juice. Cook celery (or peppers) and onions, then put in blender. Add to remaining ingredients, and bring to boil until thoroughly mixed. Put in jars and cold pack 30 minutes. Yield: 36 pints.

Barbecue Sauce

Esta Miller

15 c. tomato juice
4 c. onion
¾ c. ReaLemon juice
8 c. brown sugar
⅔ white sugar
3 c. vinegar
¾ c. mustard
⅔ c. Liquid Smoke
⅔ c. salt
2 c. Worcestershire sauce
⅓ c. paprika
2 c. Fridgex

Bring to a boil. Thicken with 2 c. Fridgex. Ladle into jars. Process 10 minutes. This is delicious for chicken pizza or serve as dip for grilled chicken strips.

Smoky Barbecue Sauce
Amy Engbretson

2 gal. tomato juice
7 Tbsp. salt
2 onions, minced fine
1 tsp. cinnamon
1 tsp. cloves
4 tsp. pepper
4 tsp. minced garlic
3½ c. white vinegar
5 Tbsp. Liquid Smoke
4 Tbsp. Worcestershire sauce
3½ c. white sugar
1 c. brown sugar
¾ c. Perma-Flo

Boil tomato juice, onion, Worcestershire sauce, and Liquid Smoke till they cook down to ⅓. Add vinegar, bring to boil again. In a bowl, combine dry ingredients and garlic thoroughly. Slowly stir into liquid. Then heat to simmer, boil for 30 minutes, stirring occasionally. Fill jars, leaving ½ inch headspace. Process 30 minutes. Yield: 12 pints.

Barbecued Deer Meat
Lorene Yoder

Barbecue Sauce:
1 c. ketchup
3 Tbsp. lemon juice
¼ c. finely chopped onion
¼ c. brown sugar
2 Tbsp. Worcestershire sauce
1 tsp. prepared mustard
¼ c. chopped celery, optional

Cut deer meat into fine chunks. Pressure cook 20 minutes at 10 lb. pressure (depending on age of deer). Discard broth. Put meat into jars only ¾ full. Add barbecue sauce to fill jar. This is the barbecue sauce I use. Or use your favorite sauce. (As many recipes as needed.)

Cheeseburger Soup to Can
Esta Miller

8 lb. hamburger, browned
7½ c. shredded carrots
10 c. diced potatoes
4 c. celery
2 c. onion
2½ c. butter
4 c. pastry flour
7½ qt. or 5 (48 oz.) cans chicken broth
2½ tsp. pepper
7½ tsp. salt

Cold pack 3 hours or 1½ hours at 10 lb. pressure. When opening a jar add: 8 oz. Velveeta cheese, 1½ c. milk, and ¼ c. sour cream.

Backyard Stew
Mary L. Troyer

8 lb. bacon, cut up
10 lb. raw hamburger
5 lb. raw chunk beef
10 qt. onion, chopped fine
1 c. Lawry's seasoned salt
10 gal. hot water
10 gal. diced potatoes
10 qt. diced carrots
6 qt. green beans
1 c. salt or to taste
¼ c. pepper
1½ (16 oz.) cont. beef soup base
10 lb. sliced Polish sausage
9 lb. cubed ham
6 qt. peas (fresh or frozen)
 Thickening:
12 c. flour
7 lg. (4.5 oz.) pkg. brown gravy mix,
  mix with cold water

We make this out in the yard in a large iron kettle. Fry bacon until brown. Add next four ingredients. Stir and fry until well done. Add 5 gallons of hot water, vegetables, salt, pepper, and soup base. Cook until veggies are soft, stirring occasionally. Add sausage, ham, and peas and the remaining 5 gallons of water. When this is boiling well, add thickening, stirring constantly. Remove kettle from heat or rake out the fire from underneath. Ladle into clean jars and pressure cook at 10 lb. for 90 minutes. Yield: 110 qt.

Favorite Chili Soup

Mrs. Marty (Esther) Miller

9 lb. hamburger
salt and pepper to taste
2 lg. onions
1 c. flour
1 gal. kidney, chili, or
   pork and beans, scant
4½ c. brown sugar
1 pkg. chili seasoning
6 qt. tomato juice
2 qt. water
3 Tbsp. salt
2 tsp. chili powder (or as desired)

Fry hamburger with salt, pepper, and onions. Add flour; mix well. Put the rest of the ingredients in a large canner. Bring to a boil; add meat mixture; boil again. Cold pack 2 hours. Makes 14 quarts.

Just Like Campbell's Tomato Soup

Miriam Schlabach

¼ c. onions
1½ c. butter
2¼ c. flour
¾ c. white sugar
¼ c. salt
1½ tsp. pepper
6 qt. tomato juice

Sauté onions in butter; stir in flour, sugar, salt, and pepper. Cook until smooth and bubbly, stirring constantly. Remove from heat. Gradually stir in tomato juice. Bring to a boil, stirring constantly. Boil for 1 minute. Fill jars and cold pack for 30 minutes or pressure can at 10 lb. for 10 minutes. To serve: gradually stir hot tomato mixture into about equal amount of cold milk, then heat to a serving temperature.

Index

Notes

Meats and Main Dishes

Vegetables and Side Dishes

Soups, Salads, and Dressings

Pies

Desserts

Cakes and Frostings

VOLUME I

Cooking with the Horse & Buggy People

A Collection of Over 600 Favorite Recipes from the Heart of Holmes County

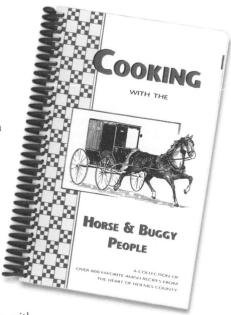

From mouth watering Amish style main dishes to kitchen dream desserts, this one has it all. Over 600 made-from-scratch recipes that please the appetite and are easy on the food budget. You'll get a whole section on canning and food preparation. The Amish, long known for their originality in the kitchen, share their favorites with you. If you desire originality, if you respect authenticity, if the Amish style cooking satisfies your taste palate—**Cooking With The Horse & Buggy People** is for you.

Contains 14 Complete Sections:
Breads, Cakes, Cookies, Desserts, Pies, Salads, Main Dishes, Soups, Cereal, Candy, Miscellaneous, Drinks, Canning, Home Remedies & Preparing Wild Game, Index.

· 5¹/₂" x 8¹/₂" · 275 pp · Spiral Bound · Laminated Cover · Convenient Thumb Index

Cooking with the Horse & Buggy People ... Item #164 ... $**12.99**

TO ORDER COOKBOOKS
Check your local bookstore or call **1-800-852-4482.**

VOLUME II

Cooking with the Horse & Buggy People

Sharing a Second Serving of Favorites
from 207 Amish Women of Holmes County, Ohio

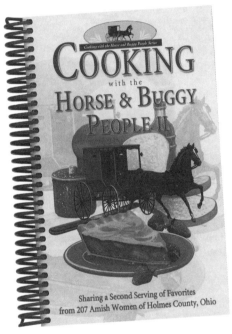

Henry and Amanda Mast, authors and compilers of *Cooking with the Horse and Buggy People Volume II* (as well as Volume I), live close to Charm, Ohio. Their home place is in the heart of the world's largest Amish community. The Masts and their friends worked countless hours in the kitchen to perfect the 600 recipes they chose to share with you.

Good food. Laughter. Compliments. Memories. That's what this new volume of *Cooking with the Horse and Buggy People* is about.

· 5¹/₂" x 8¹/₂" · 320 pp · Spiral Bound · Laminated Cover

Cooking with the Horse & Buggy People ... Item #628 ... $**12.99**

AUTHENTIC AMISH COOKING

The Wooden Spoon Cookbook

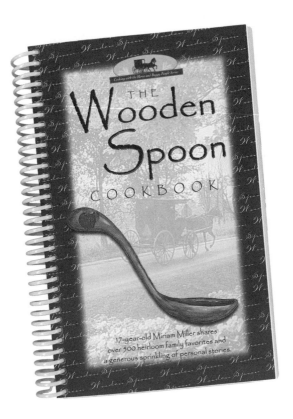

Meet 17-year-old Miriam Miller in the *Wooden Spoon Cookbook*. In addition to sharing her own, her mother's, and her grandmother's favorite recipes, Miriam shares childhood memories, stories, and personal details of her life as a young Amish girl.

· 5$^{1}/_{2}$" x 8$^{1}/_{2}$" · 194 pp · Spiral bound · Laminated cover · Double indexed

The Wooden Spoon Cookbook … Item #415 … **$10.99**

THE WOODEN SPOON

Wedding Cookbook

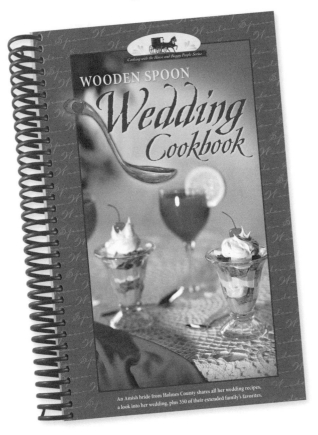

Here's a chance to experience the wedding of Amish bride Miriam Miller. Relax and sip the drink served at her bridal table. Enjoy the hearty main dishes and mouthwatering desserts served to her 500 guests. Miriam shares glimpses into the wedding as she talks about the preparation and serving of food on her special day. The icing on the cake with this cookbook is that Aden's (Miriam's husband) family have opened their recipe boxes and shared over 350 of their family favorites!

· 5¹/₂" x 8¹/₂" · Spiral bound · Laminated cover · Indexed

Wooden Spoon Wedding Cookbook … Item #005 … **$12.99**